Combat Carriers

COMBAT CARRIERS

And My Brushes with History

World War II: 1939–1946

To Todd —
with our love —
Carol 12-29-97

By Sam Sommers

Black Belt Press
Montgomery

The Black Belt Press
P.O. Box 551
Montgomery, AL 36101

 Published in the United States by the Black Belt Press, a division of the Black Belt Communications Group, Inc., Montgomery, Alabama.

Library of Congress Cataloging-in-Publication Data

Sommers, Sam, 1921-

Combat carriers : and my brushes with history : World War II, 1939-1946 / by Sam Sommers.

p. cm.

Includes bibliographical references and index.

ISBN 1-881320-92-8 (hardcover)

1. Sommers, Sam, 1921- . 2. World War, 1939-1945—Naval operations, American. 3. World War, 1939-1945—Personal narratives, American. 4. World War, 1939-1945—Campaign—Pacific Ocean. 5. Seamen—United States—Biography. 6. United States. Navy—Biography. I. Title.

D773.S66 1997

940.54'5973—dc21 97-3171

CIP

DESIGN BY RANDALL WILLIAMS

Printed in the United States of America

97 98 3 2 1

The Black Belt, defined by its dark, rich soil, stretches across central Alabama. It was the heart of the cotton belt. It was and is a place of great beauty, of extreme wealth and grinding poverty, of pain and joy. Here we take our stand, listening to the past, looking to the future.

FOR

CAROL, FRANCES, JEANNETTE, SAM, AND RUTH

CONTENTS

The author, right, in helicopter bay of the new *USS Cowpens* at her commissioning, 1991.

Preface

HISTORY, when we think of it at all, is usually considered dull stuff heard in classrooms or read in endless paragraphs from musty books. It is the account of great events in distant parts of the world, made by presidents and kings, admirals and generals, diplomats and politicians, and recorded by scholars who have dug up the facts years later.

Seldom do we think that we could ever make it ourselves, or that our little productions might be worthy of recording. But during World War II more than 70 million people in uniform worldwide,[1] as well as millions more out of uniform, made individual contributions to the story of the greatest mass event in the history of mankind.

I haven't said or written much about my war years. My memories seemed too personal, too distant, and too numerous to relate without my appearing self-serving and boring. Though many had similar experiences, I have seen no account paralleling my particular adventures: those of a junior officer aboard, and not aboard, fast aircraft carriers through much of the Pacific war. I set them out here while I have the inclination, the fractional wit, and marginal ability to put them down as my personal footnote, a tiny brush stroke on the vast canvas of World War II.

As for my ego, I didn't do anything outstanding; was awarded no medals for individual accomplishment. I just happened to be on ships with thousands of others, by the luck of the draw, through three years of historic naval action. As for the boredom factor—maybe some history *is* boring. You be the judge.

These are stories and pictures from my journey through those years, 1939–1946. The trip was completely unanticipated, unplanned, and simply happened to me in its own chronological order. That I was involved in many of the events seems impossible in retrospect. They seemed to occur steadily, routinely, and, at times, endlessly, but were typical of the events endured or enjoyed by many U.S. sailors during those years. They were my brushes with history.

Introduction

THE aircraft carrier war across the Pacific during World War II was unique in the history of warfare. In previous wars, armies had marched or been taken to land areas and had fought relatively stationary battles over extended time periods. Navies, led by the heaviest ships with the largest cannons, formed great flotillas to slug it out with their massed opponents.

The advent of airpower, aircraft carrying ships, and the control of the sky over battlefields and sections of oceans rewrote the books on military strategy and tactics. No war had ever been fought over such vast distances as the Pacific. No nation had held such immense areas as did the Japanese in 1942. Japan controlled a circle of the Pacific from the home islands to the Aleutians; south to Wake, the Marshalls, and Gilberts; south and west through the Solomons, New Guinea, the Dutch East Indies, to Burma; then east and north to the China, Korean, Manchurian coasts, and back to Japan.

Their men held their island bases, their ships supplied them, and their powerful navy of carriers, battleships, cruisers and destroyers defended their maritime empire. It is more than 3,000 miles from Tokyo to the Gilberts; more than 4,000 from the Gilberts to Singapore; and almost 3,000 from Singapore to Japan. It is more than 2,000 miles from Hawaii to the Gilberts and it is about 2,000 from our west coast our main outpost at Pearl Harbor, and at year's end 1941 Pearl Harbor was a shambles.

By May 1942, Bataan and Corregidor, in the Philippines, had fallen; General MacArthur was in Australia without men, planes, or equipment, the meager supplies of which were being sent to the war in Europe. Admiral Nimitz, from Pearl Harbor commanded a naval force, weakened by our losses on December 7, which was no match for the newer, powerful Japanese fleet. Our outlook in the Pacific was grim indeed in the early months of 1942.

Japan needed Port Moresby, New Guinea, as a final base from which to invade Australia; it needed Midway Island, a thousand miles northwest of Hawaii, to invade or neutralize those islands and Pearl Harbor. A major airfield on Guadalcanal in the Solomon Islands could cut our sea routes to Australia and New Zealand. U.S. naval power would be thrown back to our west coast.

The Japanese expansion was stopped in May and June, 1942, with the naval victories in the Coral Sea and at Midway, and the land and naval battles for Guadalcanal. The Battle of the Coral Sea ended the threat to Port Moresby; the Battle of Midway stopped the thrust toward Hawaii and Pearl Harbor. The fierce land and sea battles for Guadalcanal was the Gettysburg for the Japanese: their farthest extension of naval and military power.

The Coral Sea and Midway engagements, the first of carrier planes against ships with no visual contact between the adversary ships, were turning points of the Pacific war. But we lost the carrier *Lexington,* CV-2, in the Coral Sea; the *Yorktown,* CV-5, at Midway; the *Wasp,* CV-7, in the Solomons in August 1942; and the *Hornet,* CV-8, at the Battle of Santa Cruz in October. Of the six carriers of the Pacific fleet on December 7, 1941, none of which were in Pearl Harbor, only two remained: *Saratoga,* CV-3, and *Enterprise,* CV-6. *Saratoga,* old and slow, was often damaged and under repair, which left the *Enterprise* as our only operational carrier in late 1942 and early 1943. But help was on the way.

In 1943 the American industrial giant finally flexed its naval muscles. The new, attack aircraft carriers began arriving in the Pacific with well-trained crews and pilots, new planes, adequate anti-aircraft guns, and the newest radar and gun-control equipment. The ships were fast: all could make about 32 knots, as could the new battleships, cruisers, and destroyers which would protect them. Our naval forces were gathering to roll the Japanese back across the Pacific—strategy and tactics would develop as the enormous effort progressed and individual operations required.

The largest of the new, fast carriers was the *Essex*-class, named, as usual, for the first ship of the class, *USS Essex,* CV-9. Those ships carried about 90 planes and displaced about 35,000 tons. The figures are imprecise because of changes of armaments and missions as the war progressed. A class of smaller carriers, the *Independence*-class, was named for *USS Independence,* CVL-22. They carried about 45 planes and weighed in at about 14,000 tons. There were, eventually, nine ships of this class, which were converted from a class of cruisers under construction when the Navy desperately needed carriers in 1942. All were in action in the Pacific by late 1943 and early 1944.

The author arrived in the Pacific carrier war in the fall of '43 as a brand-new, deck and gunnery ensign aboard *USS Cowpens,* CVL-25, the fourth ship of the class. I had joined the Navy on entering Harvard College in late September 1939. The war had begun in Europe on September l, and anyone could see we would be in it sooner or later. "Join the Navy and see the world!" said the Navy poster. I knew little about the Navy but there was a great rush to get into one of the Reserve Officers Training Corps. I applied for the Navy, was accepted, and had an exciting, scary, and lucky seven years.

This is my account of my war years, 1939–1946. (The war ended in Tokyo Bay on September 2, 1945. I remained aboard my second carrier, the *Essex*-class *USS Ticonderoga,* CV-14, until May 1946, because I couldn't get home any sooner.) It is an account of my thoughts, fears, and adventures during three years aboard two attack carriers; about the training at Harvard that got me there; the anticlimactic months after the war; and of the final disposition of the carriers that helped drive the Japanese back to Japan.

My wartime recollections didn't spring, full-bodied, from my memory. My earliest ones, at Harvard, were helped by snapshots from college and some taken on a training cruise in 1941, copies of newspapers and news magazines saved from those years, and various paper memorabilia.

Navy memories were aided by my file, "jacket," of official orders and papers. I also kept a personal, very private list of dates, places, and operations in which my ships participated. The Navy, I understood, had a regulation forbidding the keeping of personal diaries or journals. Personal snapshots of naval activities were also taboo. The fear was that an enemy agent might get possession of such information, putting lives or operations at risk. Posters warned that "Loose lips sink ships"; there were tales of spies in bars, and rumors of clandestine radio transmitters sending information to German U-boats offshore. So I didn't keep a diary, log, or journal. A simple list with dates, kept securely with my personal papers would be safe from enemy agents and might prove interesting someday. It was and has because the *Cowpens* was in eight combat operations and the *Ticonderoga* was in two while I was aboard them. I didn't do anything heroic, wasn't awarded any medals for valor, but my Asiatic-Pacific ribbon has 10 battle stars on it; my Philippine Liberation ribbon has two stars; and the *Cowpens* was awarded the Navy Unit Commendation "for outstanding heroism displayed by her crew in action against enemy Japanese forces in the Pacific War Area during the periods indicated below: . . ."

Other memory-joggers were copies of newspapers describing important events. I kept a San Francisco paper, where we happened to be, describing the opening of the organizational meeting of the United Nations. A Honolulu paper headlined the end of the war in Europe. A ship's news sheet brought back the atomic bombs, events from the war's end, and plans for the occupation of Japan. Copies of official messages to the fleet reminded of the uncertainties of peace after years of combat. Organizational papers recalled *Ticonderoga*'s landing party, of which I was a member but which did not land, being formed to help occupy Japan.

My primary memory aids were augmented by four most valuable secondary sources. One was *The Story of the U.S.S. Cowpens CVL-25* (see bibliography), which was written by an unknown author, evidently from the ship's log or combat reports, in 1946. Another was the condensed, official history of the Navy in World War II by Samuel Eliot Morison, *The Two-Ocean War,* 1963, (see bibliography). A third was *The Fast Carriers,* by Clark G. Reynolds, 1968, reprinted 1992, (see bibliography). The fourth, the superb biography of Admiral Nimitz, the Commander-in-Chief Pacific Fleet, by E. B. Potter, 1976 (see bibliography). My skeletal list of operations checked, date by date and operation by operation, with the later accounts.

When I found, in the National Archives, dozens of official Navy photos taken during combat aboard *Cowpens* and *Ticonderoga,* my stomach tightened, my awareness sensors went to full alert, and it was like being at battle stations all over again, being scared, super alive, and on the edge of history in the making.

So here is my personal history of World War II: how I got there, what happened after I arrived, and what happened to the ships after the war. I can imagine how that other Ancient Mariner felt when he "stoppeth one of three." *You* must be No. 3.

Combat Carriers

First snow of the winter of 1939–40, and first snow for the author, on snowshoes in front of his freshman dormitory, Holworthy Hall.

CHAPTER 1

A Freshman at Harvard

WHEN the letter came, in the spring of 1939, admitting me to Harvard College the last thing to enter my mind would have been the thought of going to war. I was anticipating the graduation events from high school in a small southern town with the dances, dates, and excitement of such rites of passage. Graduation came on a warm May night. The summer stretched slowly through the hot three months. I got a summer job with a construction company building barracks at Craig Field, the Army Air Corps training base then under construction near my home town, Selma, Alabama.

On September 1 the world changed radically: Hitler's panzers blitzed into Poland. When Great Britain declared war on Germany on the 3rd, World War II had begun. I entered Harvard, as planned, with the Class of 1943, at the end of September, and the momentum of my life took off.

War was not unexpected. Japan had invaded Manchuria in the early thirties. The Spanish civil war had tested fascist and communist strengths. France had built its supposedly impregnable Maginot Line. Mussolini had grabbed Ethiopia. Germany had "annexed" the Rhineland, Czechoslovakia, and Austria. France and Britain, with memories of the first World War and no desire to expend more young men, were powerless against the German machine. The newspapers and newsreels recorded the perilous times—with Hitler shouting wildly at masses of storm troopers, arm extended in the Nazi salute. War had been brewing for years. Now it had erupted in Europe.

During those first, strange days in the Harvard Yard, the college seemed an exotic bazaar of options: which courses to take, what extracurricular choices to make, which teams to try out for, which newspapers and magazines to subscribe to, which laundry service to contract with, even which whiskey store to visit.

There was a new and unexpected choice: to try to get into a Reserve Officers' Training Corps (ROTC) unit with the expectation that we would be drawn into the conflict; or not volunteer, take regular courses, and hope the United States could stay out of the war. The beginning of the war abroad put the possibility of future military service into many freshman minds, including mine. There was a scramble to get into the ROTC units.

The services offered no incentives to volunteer; there were no scholarships, pay, or benefits promised. The main inducement was a negative one: what might your future be if you didn't sign up? To join a ROTC unit meant giving up an academic course each year for four years; giving up part of some summer vacations for training cruises or duties; attending training classes three times a week and one afternoon of drill; and psychologically, to prepare for a real, shooting war while trying to retain a normal college life in a nation technically at peace. Joining up would also mean having a choice of a service, becoming an officer, and not having to worry about future service decisions.

To stay out of ROTC meant getting that extra academic course each year; possibly being drafted; or, if we kept out of the war, not having to serve at all. At Harvard, as in the country, there was a variety of vehement, honest opinion about the war. The America-First isolationists, led by the heroic Charles Lindbergh, thought it should be left to the Europeans and that the U.S. should keep out at any cost. The interventionists saw the danger in a Nazi-fascist victory, seemingly inevitable at the time. The arguments didn't end until December 7, 1941.

With the war underway abroad and the strong possibility of our being drawn into it, I took the ROTC route with my parents' permission. Having had some small boat experience on the Gulf Coast, I chose the Navy. After filling out a number of forms and having a few interviews, the Navy accepted me. It was a choice I felt lucky to have made, and I was glad to have been accepted. After Pearl Harbor and our entry into the war, the Navy had about two years of training invested in my class of 38 young men. With the selective service draft getting into high gear, the Navy enlisted my class as Apprentice Seamen, USNR, to keep us in the Navy, out of the draft, and to finish our training. Our Naval ROTC class was kept in college to graduate on schedule, in June 1943. After graduation we were sent, as new Ensigns, directly to sea duty aboard combatant ships.

To this freshman in 1939, Harvard was a strange, exciting, scary place. I had come from a small high school in a small, southern town, Selma, Alabama. There were 130 in our graduating class. Here, there were about 1,900 in the freshman class alone.

There were new people, from everywhere, to meet; new methods of instruction to experience; new buildings to find (some were there before the Revolution); new activities to try; and superb facilities—gyms, playing fields, pools, boathouses, libraries, and museums to enjoy. I don't remember any formal indoctrination provided by the College, but after a few weeks I knew where my classes met, and was familiar with my new surroundings and routine.

Social adjustments were more difficult. Freshmen from all parts of the country and the world were thrown into a new social condition. We were housed in dormitories in the Yard. Meals were provided in the Harvard Union building immediately southeast of the Yard. Freshmen roomed, boarded, studied, and went to class in the Yard area for the entire first year. Unless you came from a prep school or an urban area with a number of other freshmen, you knew nobody when you arrived. Meeting new people and making new friends was difficult while adjusting to a new social environment, new study methods, new living arrangements, new recreation and athletic possibilities, and different social service and political organizations.

Then in sophomore year the entire societal picture changed—for the better. The new sophomores moved into large, residential "houses," dormitories, for upperclassmen outside the Yard. For the next three years we lived in the same group of buildings. We could make more permanent friends, eat in the house dining hall, play on house athletic teams, participate in house social activities, and order our social groupings as in a normal, small community. For three years we were in a more permanent social group.

Adding to my freshman feeling of isolation were several subjective factors. I was from a small high school in a small Southern town where I knew almost everyone and they knew me. Here, I was in an enormous class in a big city college in the North. To this newcomer, the Easterners seemed less friendly, more competitive, and more supercilious than their counterparts from the south and west. At first, I met relatively few classmates. My accent was different, my educational background different. Until I bought new clothing, like that of my peers, even my appearance was different.

My religious background was different: a minority one, almost like being a minority within a minority. I was from a Reform Jewish family from a part of the country where Jewish religious rites were observed much less formally than they were in large urban areas. I believed in God but was not too excited about expressing the belief through organized Judaism. At home I attended Sunday school and temple services only because of parental pressure. With my new-found independence, I drifted away from institutional Judaism toward a more general, inactive religious observance though remaining Jewish by affiliation. I respected all religious institutions and the people who were part of them, and still do, but wholehearted faith in their doctrines was left out of my makeup.

During my first days in the Harvard community I wondered about the extent of anti-semitism there. Like most Jews in the late 1930s, even the more passive ones in the rural South, I was aware of religious prejudice and had seen firsthand evidence of it. On a trip to Miami in the middle 1930s I had seen signs outside hotels that said "No Jews Allowed" and "Gentiles Only." Beginning in about 1937 the first Jewish refugees began arriving in Selma from Germany, driven out by Nazi persecution. They were the lucky ones. The persecutions and the existence of concentration camps was of public knowledge, but the magnitude of the Holocaust wasn't evident to me until the end of the war.

I can remember, dimly from childhood, the presidential election of 1928. Al Smith, a Roman Catholic Democrat, ran against the Republican, Herbert Hoover. The Klan, politically powerful at the time and a threat to any minority, was vehemently anti-Catholic and anti-Smith, even in usually Democratic Alabama. Remarks like, "The Pope will be running the country," and "Rome will replace Washington as the capital" were some of the milder anti-Smith remarks, not heard again until John Kennedy, '40, ran for president in 1960.

My expectation of overt religious prejudice at Harvard was completely unfulfilled, institutionally or individually. It was the most open, diverse community I could have imagined, though some social limitations because of religion could be felt. Many differences of opinion, politics, races, religions, nationalities, social mores, and lifestyles were in evidence and were tolerated. There were groups of young Democrats, Republicans, and Socialists. There was even a Young Communist League. To my knowledge, neither racial nor gender contentions had appeared on the social or political scenes.

There was one familiar face in my freshman melange. He was (and is) Jerry Siegel, '40, a senior who lived in Kirkland House. We had grown up next door to one another in Selma, and though a few years older, he had been a close friend from childhood. Jerry invited me to meals and other events in Kirkland and couldn't have been more helpful. When the time came to move out of the Yard, sophomore year, I chose Kirkland, was admitted, and though Jerry had departed, my three years there were pleasant ones.

I didn't feel at home with my studies, activities, and social grouping until my sophomore year in Kirkland. There I realized that most people had individual hang-ups—a consciousness that they were different in some way: financially, educationally, physically, ethnically, religiously, or some such. I also found that among civil people, the differences were unimportant. What counted were integrity, normal moral decency, and personal relationships within the subgroups—organizations, teams, and committees that one became involved in. The Harvard method, of putting diverse individuals from different backgrounds together and letting them sort out their relationships civilly, within the community, seemed to work. "Veritas," Latin for "truth," was on the Harvard seal.

By my sophomore year I found that I could do the academic work well enough to appreciate and enjoy it. I was elected to the Kirkland house committee and served on it for the next three years; I brought in dates for house dances and football weekends, and played on several of the house, intramural athletic teams.

I had been a mediocre athlete in high school. On a scale of one to ten I would have rated myself a four. Still, my second home in Selma, from about age eight, had been the YMCA. There we learned to play various games and in winter swam in a heated, indoor pool; but mainly we played basketball, from peewee leagues until we entered high school. In summer we went to a "Y" camp, with no electricity or plumbing, on a creek bank 15 miles from town. We had a great Y director, Paul Grist, of the highest character and excellent athletic ability. Though unappreciated by his charges at the time, he coached all the athletic teams and, with his wife, ran the camp, while providing a remarkable role model with his outstanding, unassuming traits of character. When successive groups of Y basketball teams reached high school, the high school coach had only to show them where the court was. Most of the preparation had been done at the Y. But I wasn't one of those pointed at the court. I enjoyed playing basketball but was a second-stringer, a mainspring of the B-team.

Baseball was a big part of my childhood. Selma had a professional team, the Cloverleafs, in the Southeastern League with Mobile, Montgomery, Pensacola, Meridian, and Columbus, Georgia. The father of one of my close, neighborhood friends, Maurice "Brother" Bloch, owned the team. Mr. Bloch, at the suggestion of our Y director, allowed the Y to organize a "Knothole Club." Members were issued a club pass, were admitted free to all home games, had to sit in the last bleacher section along the right field foul line, and were expected to cheer for the Cloverleafs. We hollered our heads off. Other requirements for membership were a good moral character, passing grades in school, and, ugh, attendance of Sunday, or Saturday, school.

Since we attended all home games, we soon knew the names, batting averages, pitching records, and some of the personal habits of the players. Most chewed tobacco, some had bad tempers and used pretty foul words, some were slow, and others were "greased lightning." We all had our own gloves and had sandlot games in side yards at home. Our balls and bats were given us by the Cloverleaf players. Gloves came from a local hardware store, their "pockets" carefully shaped and kept soft from year to year with neatsfoot oil. Scuffed baseballs and cracked bats from the ball park were repaired with friction tape and would last all summer.

Many "knotholers" would get to the park, with their gloves, an hour or two before game time with the hope of warming up with a player. Often, before enough players arrived, the earliest players would let us play catch with them, or as we called it, "warm them up." Those were "seventh heaven" moments. We'd get 80 feet or so away and the player would throw the ball easily to us. We'd fire it back briskly so the player would know he'd picked a "live" kid. As the player warmed up he would throw harder. I can still feel the delicious sting as the ball popped into the pocket of my glove. It was a disappointment when other players would arrive to warm up and my player would say, "That's enough, kid. Come back tomorrow."

But I didn't play baseball in high school. When spring and warm weather came it was time to go swimming and knock a golf ball around the local course. In my junior year of high school the school started a track team. I finally learned the special rhythm of running the high hurdles and could cover 110 yards in a not abysmal time. I was a mediocre high jumper, and, since few boys wanted to run the mile, I was a miler. I was awarded my "S" in track so, for the record, I was a varsity athlete in high school. My track experience proved useful when I got to college.

High school football was out of the question. I weighed about 120 pounds and was a stringy five-feet-eight. I wasn't about to be a third-string defensive end to be flattened by the big, varsity hulks, some of whom had been in high school an extra year or two.

At Harvard in the fall of 1939, athletics seemed an ideal extracurricular activity. Like a lot of other freshmen, I had no idea how much studying was necessary to stay in school. My friend Jerry had told me how tough it was freshman year. Not wanting the shame of flunking out, or as Harvard so delicately put it, "having my connection with the College severed . . . ," I hit the books. Athletics wouldn't take too much time. The hour exams in November were the first, terrible tests. My schedule until November had me going to classes in the mornings, Navy drill or studying most of the afternoon, except for a couple of hours for some kind of required athletics, and more studying at night. Football games on fall Saturdays, followed by going downtown for a meal or movie filled my freshman fall weeks. I did okay in November and relaxed.

With about a hundred other freshmen, I tried out for freshman basketball in Hemenway Gym. My name wasn't on the list to return. I tried for the crew at Newell Boat House. A dozen of us at a time rowed in a flat-bottomed barge. Again, I wasn't on the list to return. Fall track activities were limited to cross-country training. My mile-run experiences in high school told me that I wasn't cut out for distance running, so I decided to wait until late winter to try the track route.

My freshman fall brought some new athletic experiences. To fill my athletic requirement, an hour or two a week, I learned to balance in and row a single-seated wherry from Weld Boat House. I never was graduated to a single scull. I played enough squash to enjoy it, and swam exercise laps in the Indoor Athletic Building pool.

In February 1940, when the first notices for a freshman track team appeared, I reported at Dillon Field House on Soldiers' Field. I was directed to find the freshman track coach, Bill Neufield, who was checking out some freshman prospects in a garage-like, brick building near Briggs Cage. The narrow building, possibly Cary Cage, contained a sawdust pit for high and broad jumping and another pit for pole vault practice, all sheltered from the snowy, winter weather. Coach Neufield, a kindly, experienced coach of about 50, let me try out with a few high jumps and a few 40-yard hurdles runs in the briggs. The '43 freshman track team must have been desperate for bodies, for the coach told me I could practice with the team and gave me the practice schedule. I discovered, quickly, that track practice was mostly a matter of jogging laps, on the banked, wooden track in Briggs Cage in winter, and on the cinder track inside the stadium in good weather. Though I made the

Approaching the high jump bar in stadium warm-up.

team, I didn't have many first-place finishes, but did place and show a few times and was on the list of participants on a few Boston sport pages and in *The Crimson*.

Being on a varsity team had its pleasant perks. Before big track meets we ate at the Varsity Club training table and were given small steaks for energy, a delightful contrast to the dining hall food. We were issued uniforms, sweats, socks, jocks, and shoes, and the athletic department did the laundry. Road trips were great too. We were taken by bus to Andover, Exeter, and Yale. Other teams came to meets at Harvard. The track team was THE highlight of my freshman year. I was awarded freshman numerals at the end of the year and, though I knew I wasn't a real athlete, basked in my brief moment of glory. I wasn't awarded another track letter until my senior year. The certificate was at home when I arrived on leave from the Pacific in December 1944. It wasn't such a big deal then.

CHAPTER 2

Navy Training at Harvard

IN THE fall of 1939, naval ROTC wasn't just another college course. It met three times a week, with one afternoon session of drill or an occasional field trip to the Boston Navy Yard to board real Navy ships. The Navy issued us about $200 as a uniform allowance, measured us, ordered the uniforms, delivered them, and we returned the allowances as payment for them. This procedure, I suppose, was to accustom us to the time, after commissioning, when we received a similar amount as a real allowance to buy our own uniforms independently. The uniforms were regular, officers' navy blue, without sleeve stripes to indicate rank and with midshipmen's insignia on the caps. We wore them at our weekly drill sessions for the next four years.

The Navy classes were different from the academic ones, technical and practical among the liberal arts. They would be useful if we went to war but with the nation still at peace, were we wasting our time, effort, and money? There were no "crip" courses, but because of their subject matter the Navy classes were easier than the usual academic instruction. We understood that this was one series of courses we had to master. Any show of patriotism was considered corny at the time, but I think the NROTC classes had some of it, and secretly we were proud to be a part of the nation's armed services.

Our naval science classes were held in a white marble building that once housed the school of architecture. The building, no longer there, was just inside the northeast fence of the Yard on the site of Canaday Hall. The classes were taught thoroughly and fairly by active duty Navy officers. Two of our instructors, Lieutenants Black and Abele, were killed in action later in the war.

Our instruction included subjects vital to the training of prospective naval officers. They were taught with problems worked on paper with the navigational tools of the day: dividers, compass roses, parallel rulers, and slide rules. The courses included piloting and seamanship (maneuvering a ship using landmarks on shore); celestial navigation using Bowditch on navigation, star elevations from a sextant, a chronometer, and the current Nautical Almanac; and naval strategy and tactics from a classic work by Admiral Mahan. A most useful instruction was in the use of a maneuvering board. The portable device allowed us to compute the relative movements of ships or aircraft in time, direction, and speed to position one unit in relation to another. Since naval war ultimately boils down to the relative, mechanical movement of physical objects—ships and planes—the use of this speedy means of solving relative movement problems mathematically and graphically proved most useful.

General information came from a Navy Department publication called *The Watch Officer's Guide*. Two of its items stick in my memory: if two ships are approaching and the bearing (direction of the line sight) between them doesn't change they will eventually collide. (The bearing can be changed by altering your course, speed, or both.) The instruction is still useful. I use it frequently while driving a golf cart. Another recommended forehandedness. To be forehanded was to anticipate situations or conditions. The anticipation might make a solution more effective. Sometimes it did, sometimes it didn't, but it was suggested in the textbook.

In addition to our classroom courses, the Navy took us on field trips, put us through rigorous physical training, and taught us the discipline of close-order drill. At the end of each year, the NROTC classes had a formal review on Soldiers' Field, the athletic fields across the river. President Conant and an assortment of deans were invited; the Commandant of the Naval District headquartered in Boston and his staff were there, as were the Commander of the Harvard Naval Science unit and our instructors. (See photo.)

To prepare for the review, we drilled inside Memorial Hall in our regulation winter uniforms under regular, stiff-visored caps with changeable navy-colored covers for winter and white for summer. In black

Naval ROTC unit drilling in Memorial Hall. This drill was a final rehearsal for the official review to be held on the Soldier's Field baseball diamond. (Photo from *LIFE,* May 5, 1941)

Naval review, Soldier's Field, May 6, 1943. First unit is of WAVE graduates; second, of male officer graduates; third and following, the Harvard Naval ROTC classes. Navy band plays at right. Spectators, under umbrellas, at corner of baseball stands, at left. (Photo from *Boston Daily Record,* May 7, 1943.)

shoes, white shirts, and black ties, we marched with Springfield rifles of World War I vintage. Our drill instructor was a short Marine sergeant who was permanently assigned to our unit. He tried to be rough, tough, and savage, like a proper Marine drill instructor, but he wasn't. He seemed to like his job and didn't want to jeopardize it by chewing us out too badly. But chew us he did.

One of my minor triumphs—I can't recall any major ones—occurred at one of our drills during senior year. The sergeant had several seniors, including me, come out of the ranks and march a squad around the floor of the hall. To show us what was expected, the sergeant chalked an "X" on the floor in front of the man at the extreme left end of the squad. Then he marched the group around the hall and stopped them in the exact places from which they had started. The proper man was behind the "X." We were to do as the sergeant had and stop the man behind the mark.

At Naval Review, 1943: Edward Garrison receives navigation proficiency award from Admiral R. A. Theobald, Commandant, First Naval District, Boston. To his right, Captain G. N. Barker, Professor of Naval Science and Tactics. To his right, our Marine drill sergeant. At extreme left, the author, battalion adjutant, with list of award winners. (Photo from *Boston Daily Record,* May 7, 1943.)

When a senior would march the men around and fail to stop them at the "X," the sergeant, with much bellowing of insults and assorted dramatics, would take them around to the proper place. Fortunately I wasn't the first, second, or third senior to have to do the drill. After watching the sergeant march the group a few times, I suddenly got the picture. The afternoon sun, shining through the clerestory windows, made several bright spots on the floor. The sergeant was using certain spots to order his turns and final halt. When my turn came I used the same spots and stopped the group behind the "X" as if I did it every day. The incident, I think, made me the battalion adjutant at the final review.

We were taken, in uniform, on a number of timely field trips. One afternoon we were bused to the Navy Yard in Charlestown. Some British

Seniors, Harvard Naval ROTC, Cambridge, 1943. From left, front row: Howard Oedel, Caleb Loring, Philip Williams, Ken Munzert, Shanks, Frank Dunham, Jim Wolf, and Dave Place. MIddle: Ed Garrison, Harold Small, Bill Latimer, T. P. Spencer, Morris Gray, Stuyvesant Fish, Rufus Walker, Harry O'Hare, and Mal Miller. Rear: Henry Campbell, Charles Wright, Gerard Coster, Bollay, William Woodward, Thomas Redmond, Oliver Ames, Robert Townsend, Sam Sommers, Al Levine, and Nat Blanchard. (Ten others were not pictured.)

warships were in port, possibly for repair or supplies during the Lend-Lease period before Pearl Harbor. The purpose of the trip, probably, was to show us the newest secret weapon: radar. As we approached the ships, on foot down a pier, the metal bed-spring-like devices on the masts were pointed out. The devices revolved and transmitted radio waves, which, when bounced from a target and returned to the antenna would give distance, direction, and altitude of the target. All this in any kind of weather, or in darkness, at the speed of light—the constant speed of radio waves. The information could be fed electrically to aim antiaircraft guns ahead of a target. Another surface radar was used to "draw" on a screen to scale shorelines, other ships, or other surface features in fog or darkness. RADAR is short for Radio Direction And Ranging. The device, an Anglo-American development, was top-secret equipment of tremendous value to the allied war effort.

Another trip from the Navy Yard was my first aboard a U.S. warship. The ship, a new destroyer, was going out for a day of sea trials. The trials included speed and maneuvering events; that ship could move and did. The details of the day are dim, after all the years, but I recall vividly the power of that ship and the smell of that power.

We were taken in small groups to various parts of the ship: the operating bridge; the wardroom; the bow, with its anchor chains, windlasses, and five-inch gun turrets; amidships, where the torpedo tubes could be turned outboard for firing; the stern, where the depth charges were stored; the living compartments and mess decks; and the power center of the machine, the main engine compartments.

We were well clear of the harbor and headed to sea when my group entered the engine space. The compartments were brightly lighted and completely filled with machinery in full-throated operation. We walked on grating catwalks which threaded down through the steamy maze. Every now and then a sailor, shouting above the roar, would tell us what we were looking at: boilers, turbines, reduction gears, steam and condenser lines. Finally we reached the main control area. Dungaree-clad sailors in white T-shirts and caps checked dials, turned valves, and controlled the enormous horsepower as directed from the bridge and supervised by the engineering officer of the watch.

My main memory of the engine room, and of the entire ship, is of the odor of fuel oil. It was not the dirty smell of burned exhaust from a bus; it was the slick, sick-sweet smell of fresh petroleum. The day, as I recall, was overcast, spitting rain, the sea with a light chop. On outside decks we hung on to rails or lifelines as the ship leapt along. But wherever we went—bow, stern, or below—there was the fuel oil smell. The entire ship vibrated with the power it produced.

Another sea trip, from June 12 to June 24, 1941, was longer. It was a summer training cruise off the New England coast. I found a set of snapshots taken during the voyage, most with descriptions written on the backs, so many details are recalled. Our ship was the *USS St. Augustine*, a former private yacht that had been converted to a coastal patrol and training ship. Handwriting on the back of a photo of the ship says that it was 272 feet long; it had a beam of 36 feet; the bridge was 25 feet above the water; it had 3600 horsepower, 1800 for each shaft and propeller, and a turboelectric drive. As I recall, it was slow, unable to make more than 15 or 16 knots. It had two small guns, with two or three-inch projectiles, one forward and one aft. A group picture shows about 25 of us, with one officer, Lieutenant Cooper, and Chief Petty Officer Benjamin.

For the cruise, we were issued standard, white, seamen's uniforms with "R.O.T.C., U.S.N.R. HARVARD" stenciled across the chests. Instead of plain white sailor hats, ours had a blue band around the rim. Our clothing—an extra uniform, T-shirts, shorts, and socks—and toilet articles were stowed, with the sea bag we brought them aboard in, in small lockers in our living compartment. We slept in hammocks which were stowed in the daytime and were slung to hooks in the overhead at night.

I had never slept in a hammock before, nor have I since, so getting used to one took a few hours the first night. A hammock is least uncomfortable when strung as tightly and as horizontally as possible. But

Our ROTC unit sailed aboard the *USS St. Augustine* on a training cruise, June 12–24, 1941.

Aboard *USS St. Augustine*, 1941. From left, Thaxter Spencer, Bill Wood, Sam Sommers. Below: Harvard sailors practice rowing under fantail overhang of anchored *USS St. Augustine* during 1941 cruise.

when slung under an overhead that is covered with pipes and conduits . . . If you get it too tight your face is too close to the pipes, some of which were hot, if too loose your back is gone by morning. Slinging a hammock properly, we found, is an art of its own.

My snapshots show us doing navigation problems with a sextant, receiving lectures sitting at the base of the after gun, and listening to Al Levine, '43, play his accordion. I also recall holystoning (scrubbing with a block of pumice on a mop handle) the teak decks, then hosing, barefooted, the milky residue overboard. Bell-bottomed trousers rolled up easily, and stayed up. Those ancient British sailors had some practical ideas.

We fired the guns a few times, stood lookout watches in daylight, dark, fog, and, in slickers, rain. Food was eaten in the crews' mess, and we were subjected to many inspections of our living quarters and lockers.

After several foggy nights, with the fog horn sounding incessantly,

Chief Petty Officer Benjamin on fantail of *St. Augustine,* 1941. To the chief's right is Al Levine, '43, with his accordion.

Right: One Harvard sailor, with sextant, takes sun sight while the other records time and angle, aboard *St. Augustine*, 1941.

Below: *HMS Rodney* from *St. Augustine*, 1941. *Rodney* is headed for the Boston Navy Yard after participating in the sinking of the German battleship *Bismarck*. Note *Rodney's* three turrets are forward of her fire control tower, none aft. Cables in foreground are "degaussing" (anti-magnetic) equipment, to protect *St. Augustine* from magnetic mines.

we anchored off Bar Harbor, Maine. Liberty parties were allowed ashore and several of us were met by a local couple with a car. After taking us home to most welcome sandwiches, they drove us around the beautiful, tree-covered Mt. Desert Island area. Rocky hills rose directly from the cold bays, and forested islands were scattered near the shore. The public road frequently went under the private bridges and roads of the Henry Ford estate. After a couple of hours of sight-seeing our hospitable hosts returned us to the landing.

On the way back toward Boston, the *St. Augustine* was sent to a point off Portsmouth, New Hampshire, where one of our submarines had sunk. The *USS Squalus,* on a trial run in 1939, had suffered a mechanical mishap and had come to rest on the ocean floor under several hundred feet of water. News stories said that during a dive the boat's main air induction valve had remained open and enough water had entered the hull to sink it. Many of the crew were rescued with a new rescue bell lowered from a salvage ship, but a number of men in flooded compartments were lost. When the *St. Augustine* arrived, several tugs and salvage ships were working to raise the submarine, and possibly to test new rescue devices that were being developed.

The *St. Augustine* was, I suppose, sent to the area to let us observe an actual Navy salvage operation in progress, but there was little to see and after a day or two, our ship was sent northeastward to meet and escort *HMS Rodney* to Boston.

The *Rodney,* a British battleship, had been in the action, just completed, that sank the German battleship, *Bismarck,* off the coast of France. *Rodney* was headed for the Boston Navy Yard for repairs and possibly a load of lend-lease armaments. After a few hours of steaming, we sighted the ship headed southwesterly.

It was a strange looking ship. Most battleships had two turrets forward of the superstructure and one or two aft. *Rodney* had three turrets forward—one at maindeck level; a second behind it, a turret level above the first; and a third aft of the second on the maindeck level. Aft of the three turrets was the superstructure, a stack, a mast, and the ship's stern. The ship appeared to have had its rear third sliced off.

After an exchange of signal-light messages, we turned to a parallel course as an escort. The engagement with the *Bismarck* hadn't affected *Rodney's* speed. She seemed to be moving at a steady 20 knots or so. We couldn't keep up with our escortee. The *Rodney,* at its steady pace, soon left us, embarrassingly, behind and steamed toward Boston unescorted.

A classmate told me that later in the war, the *St. Augustine* was torpedoed off the Florida coast by a German submarine. It must have gone down like a stone. It had no armor plating, watertight compartments, or submarine detection gear. It was slow and feebly armed. It had been built as a pleasure yacht and had been converted, unsuitably, to a coastal patrol vessel. I hope there were at least a few survivors.

THE ORDINARY, day-to-day, unmilitary life at Harvard in those years was memorable. Famous people seemed simply to appear. During the presidential campaign of 1940, Wendell Willkie, the Republican nominee, spoke from an open automobile near Harvard Square. Seated in his car while he spoke were Mrs. Willkie and Leverett Saltonstall, Harvard '14, then Governor of Massachusetts and later U.S. Senator. President Franklin Roosevelt, '04, appeared in the Boston Garden downtown.

At the 1943 freshman smoker, an annual entertainment for the freshman class, the program included Cab Calloway and his orchestra; Rochester of the Jack Benny radio program; stars from a musical playing in Boston, including Jimmy Durante, Ray Bolger, and Jane Froman; master of ceremonies Colonel Stoopnagle, a nationally known radio comedian of the time; and '43's own Ray Guild. Duke Ellington and Vaughn Monroe appeared at nightclubs in the area and sometimes played at house dances.

Once when I was entering the main door of Widener Library, who should come out but Frederic March, the movie star. He was in a play downtown, and, as it happened, I had seen the play a few days before. I told him I had enjoyed his performance and he thanked me cordially. Pretty heady stuff for a freshman from a small Southern town.

I had another memorable encounter on the Widener steps one snowy evening. I had come out of the main door just after dark. It was

Wendell Willkie campaigning near Harvard Square, fall 1940.

very cold and the wooden steps were covered with drifted snow near the handrails. A very old man, with a white beard and a dark overcoat and hat was creeping down the steps holding for dear life to the right hand railing.

I took his thin, left forearm and we made it, slowly and safely, to ground level. I asked if I could help him home, or wherever. He thanked me and said someone would pick him up in a car in a few minutes. Then he asked, "Do you know who I am?"

"No, sir," I said.

"I'm A. B. Hart; I was in the class of 1880, same class as Teddy Roosevelt."

Being a history major I knew who A. B. Hart was; Albert Bushnell Hart was a well-known historian and retired Harvard professor. Soon, a car stopped before us; I helped him in, and off he went. My encyclopedia[2] says that he was born in 1854, was a Harvard professor for many years,

Professor Albert Bushnell Hart, Class of 1880, in his study. He was a friend and supporter of his classmate, Theodore Roosevelt. (Photo from *LIFE,* May 5, 1941)

was a prolific writer of history, and was a longtime friend and supporter of his classmate, Theodore Roosevelt. He died on June 16, 1943.

Well known names in the Harvard history department of my years were Professors Roger Merriman, Arthur Schlesinger, Sr., Frederick Merk, and Paul Buck. All knew their subjects forward and backward and delivered their lectures with the unassuming ease and authority of years of study and experience. Best known of all at Harvard was, of course, President James B. Conant.

Distant contacts with Mr. Conant are pleasant memories of those years. One of the first orientation meetings of the Class was with Mr. Conant. It was the only time the entire class ever met in the same place at the same time. Almost all of us sat down on the swept, oiled floor of the main dining room of the Union building. Except for his welcoming remarks, I can't remember what he said, but he must have referred to outbreak of the war in Europe, a subject that was a cloud on all of our horizons.

Later during freshman year, Mr. and Mrs. Conant had groups of us to their home for afternoon tea. It must have been a major undertaking considering their other duties, but by the end of the year the entire class had been invited to their teas. The Conants lived in a large, brick Georgian house on Quincy Street, in the southeast part of the Yard. After our entry into the war, the Conants moved out and the mansion was used as offices for the military and naval science departments.

At the tea I attended, the Conants made small talk to make us feel at home. When my turn came and I told him I was from Alabama. He said he had been in "Ahlabahma" only once, on a train on the way to New Orleans. Mine wasn't the only odd accent at Harvard. As Mark Twain said, "I have traveled more than anyone else, and I have noticed that even the angels speak English with an accent." Mr. Conant stopped in Alabama after the war. In the late 1940s he spoke to an alumni meeting in Birmingham.

Another contact with Mr. Conant was on Monday, December 8, 1941. Japanese carrier planes had blasted Pearl Harbor on Sunday afternoon, Cambridge time. Posters on bulletin boards Monday morning announced that President Conant would address the University at 11 o'clock in Sanders Theater, in Memorial Hall. As I recall the scene, a large loudspeaker was at one side of the stage front, a lectern stood in the center, and a number of empty chairs made a line behind the lectern. At the appointed time, Mr. Conant and a number of deans and officials entered and took their seats. President Roosevelt's "Date in Infamy" speech to Congress came from the speaker. Congress declared war against the Japanese. Mr. Conant made some serious remarks, doubtlessly about the role of the University and each of us in the effort to come. We filed out of the building, somberly aware of what the country, and we, were facing.

In early May 1943, the NROTC seniors received orders to our first ships. I was to report, as a newly commissioned Ensign, to the Philadelphia Navy Yard on June 14th, "for temporary active duty awaiting transportation to the vicinity in which the *USS Cowpens,* CVL-25, may be. . . ." Since I had finished my last exam about May 18th and had to report in Philadelphia on June 14th, I didn't wait in Cambridge for graduation day.[3] With the permission of Harvard and the Navy, I went home. My commissioning as an Ensign, USNR, was to have been done at graduation, May 27th that year. The ceremony required my swearing of the oath of allegiance and receiving my commissioning certificate. My Navy records show that on May 26, 1943, 1 was discharged as an Apprentice Seaman, USNR, to be commissioned on May 27th. I took my oath at the Headquarters of the Eighth Naval District, New Orleans, on the 27th. I found my Harvard diploma in the mail when I arrived home, on leave, in late December 1944. I couldn't read it. It was in Latin! I could make out the name, "Samuelem Alexandrum Sommers." It was signed, "Jacobus Bryant Conant, Praeses."

I left Selma on June 11, 1943, for Philadelphia and stopped off in Washington enroute to visit my junior-year roommate. I had three roommates at Harvard, two of whom were naval officers later. My freshman roommate was Sheal Becker, of Fort Thomas, Kentucky. I had a single room in Kirkland House my sophomore year. My roommate my junior year was a senior, the late Bernard Fensterwald, '42, from Nashville, Tennessee, who was, in 1943, a Navy officer stationed in Washington. My senior-year roommate was Jim Wolf, '43, from Albion, Nebraska, an NROTC classmate who was traveling to the *USS Enterprise,* CV-6, at about the time I was reporting aboard *Cowpens.*

After spending the night in the house Fensterwald and several junior officers were renting, I went to the main Navy Department building where he worked to meet him for lunch. In 1943, pre-Pentagon days, the Navy headquarters was in a series of low, "temporary," World War I buildings on Constitution Avenue near the present site of the Vietnam Memorial. The main entrance to the Department was a row of about 10 wooden doors placed in the central building facing the avenue. To keep entrance traffic orderly, pipe standards, waist high and about 30 feet long, marked lanes from the sidewalk to each doorway.

I phoned my friend from the information desk in the lobby and he came from his office to meet me. It was a nice day, so we went outside and stood, in uniform, in one of the lanes "shooting the breeze," a wartime term for idle talking. Suddenly there was an irritated "Hurrummmph" behind us and I looked around to see arms full of gold braid, a foot of chest ribbons, and Admiral Ernest J. King, the CominCh (Commander-in-Chief, U.S. Fleet) and CNO (Chief of Naval Operations) himself. He seemed nine feet tall and his cap visor was covered with "scrambled eggs." He was waiting impatiently for us to clear the lane so he could go by. I don't remember saluting, as we had been taught, but I do remember going under a pipe, on the double or maybe the triple. Two days on active duty and I had already inconvenienced the Big Boss himself. What a start for my naval career.

CHAPTER 3

The *Cowpens* at Philadelphia

BEFORE and during World War II, the Navy had a simple system for naming its ships. Aircraft carriers were named for historic battles or former Navy ships: e.g. the *Lexington, Yorktown, Enterprise, Hornet, and Wasp.* Battleships were named for states, cruisers for cities, destroyers for people, and submarines for fish.

The battle of Cowpens was a particularly savage U.S. victory fought during the Revolution at some cow pens near what is now Spartanburg, South Carolina. In the early 1940s, when we needed fleet aircraft carriers quickly, the Navy took a class of light cruisers already under construction and changed them to a class of light carriers. The *Independence*-class of CVLs (C-carrier, V-aircraft, L-light) was named for the first ship of the class, the *USS Independence,* CVL-22. The *USS Cowpens* was CVL-25.

To widen and stabilize the slim cruiser hulls, "blisters," about four feet thick amidships, were built along each side of each hull, tapering into the bows and sterns. The original propulsion machinery was left in the ships, making them as fast as any light cruiser. Top speed was about 32 knots, or about 35 miles-per-hour. They were 623 feet long; flight decks were slightly less than the hull lengths and were 109 feet wide; the ships had displacements of 13,000 tons; and had drafts, loaded, of 26 feet.[4] Above the engine rooms were two decks of living spaces, a hangar deck, two aircraft elevators, a steam-powered catapult compartment, and a flight deck. Four smokestacks were routed up the right (starboard) side of the ship, far enough outboard so as not to interfere with the wings of planes. A small island structure, resembling a child's large tree house with a mast, yardarms, and antennas, was erected forward of the stacks. Each ship could operate about 45 planes, divided as desired among Grumman F6F fighters, Douglas SBD dive bombers, and Grumman TBF torpedo bombers. The new class of carriers was small and didn't look like much, but they were fast, maneuverable, and could operate efficiently with the larger fast carriers, battleships, cruisers, and destroyers.

Former President Bush was flying a TBF torpedo bomber, from *San Jacinto,* CVL-30, when he was shot down. Former President Ford was a junior deck officer on *Monterey,* CVL-26. The CVLs were in every action in the Pacific from early 1943 until the end of the war. (See appendix.) *Cowpens* was the first carrier to enter Tokyo Bay, although I was on another carrier outside the bay, the *Essex*-class *USS Ticonderoga,* CV-14, by then. Many were damaged by enemy action. The *Princeton,* CVL-23, was bombed, set afire, and sunk. All of them, by their natures, had crashes, accidents, and fires. The *Cowpens,* through many operations and air attacks, was never scratched by enemy action, I am happy and thankful to report.

On June 14, 1943, I reported, as ordered, to the Commandant of the naval district at the Philadelphia Navy Yard. The *Cowpens* was receiving her final fitting-out at a dock in the yard so I didn't have to travel far to find her. After having my orders endorsed in the Commandant's office, I was directed to a bus that would take me to the ship. Being the only passenger on the bus, I took a seat opposite the driver. After bumping over rail tracks and winding among buildings for a while, we stopped in an open area. "This is as close as I can go," said the driver. "There she is, over there."

I got off with my two suitcases and couldn't see anything that looked like a ship. When I discovered that the *Cowpens* was an aircraft carrier, after receiving my orders in Cambridge, I assumed that she would look like the carriers we saw in the newsreels: a long, graceful flat top with a pyramidal island-structure amidships starboard side.

When I finally saw what had to be the *Cowpens,* my heart sank. Among the cranes, platforms, and masts was what appeared to be a horizontal, factory-like building with four short smokestacks in a row on the roof. An unfinished water tower, the island structure, was at the left of the stacks. When I got closer, the ship seemed covered with pipes, wires, hoses, and workmen, all going in different directions. The sound of riveting echoed from the hangar deck and welding torches flashed irregular blue signals. I went up two flights of wooden steps, across a short gangway to the hangar deck, saluted the quarterdeck and the officer-of-the-deck as we had been taught, and reported aboard.

The Delaware River, where it passed Philadelphia, stank. The river was the drain for all the industrial and chemical plants along it in Pennsylvania and New Jersey. In 1943, living on the river must have been like living inside a paper mill. Silver coins in your pocket, if they weren't spent quickly, turned green. Clips of fountain pens, belt buckles, braid on uniforms and caps turned green and then black.

The *Cowpens* was moored to pier in the river. The ships' company of officers and men lived aboard. The airgroup—planes, pilots, crewmen and maintenance men—was at a naval air station 50 miles inland in Pennsylvania. I was assigned to a cabin, with three other junior officers, two decks below the hangar deck on the port (left) side of the ship. There were no portholes; only the thin steel wall of the compartment, the light cruiser armor, and the void space of the "blister" separated us from the water. We were below the waterline in "torpedo junction," as we called it, hoping the words wouldn't be prophetic.

One of the junior officers on the *Cowpens,* Ed Stern, from Chicago, had married a Selma girl, Jeanne Cadden. I had heard he had been assigned to the ship, so I knew one person when I reported aboard. Other new friends were Bill Guthrie, from Iowa; Bruce Telfer, Chicago; and Ken Maudsley, from Wisconsin. All have died since the war except Maudsley, whom I have had the pleasure of seeing at a *Cowpens* reunion. I have seen the former Jeanne Cadden occasionally during the years, when she visited in Selma.

The Sterns and several of the other married officers had a small social group. They lived in inexpensive apartments in Philadelphia and would invite me and other bachelor officers occasionally for drinks or potluck supper. As I recall, we were off duty every other night and free to come and go as we pleased, to be aboard ship for muster the next morning.

Like most unattached young men, recreation to me meant going to the "in" bar, having a few drinks, meeting some girls, and seeing what

***USS Cowpens* before receiving camouflage paint in 1944. Note four small smokestacks at left of island and "blister" on hull amidships.**

might happen next. Nothing much did, and at this time I wouldn't admit it if it had, but the chase was fun and exciting enough for some macho stories aboard ship the next day.

Our starting point was the Bellevue-Stratford Hotel bar, downtown. After dark the Bellevue bar was filled with officers and enlisted men, soldiers, sailors, WAVES, WACS, and an assortment of women and girls, all drinking, partying, and scouting. One of our group, an Ensign from Los Angeles, had an enviable attainment: he attracted girls like honey attracts ants. There was nothing unusual about his appearance: he was of medium height, dark hair, plain features; the kind of man they recruit in spy novels because you wouldn't look at him twice. But let him walk into a bar and, bingo, in five minutes he would be surrounded by girls, all competing for his attention. One theory was that he acted so helpless that the women wanted to take care of him. It never worked for the rest of us. He seldom returned to the ship with us. The next day he would hint at tall tales with a disgusting diffidence.

An aircraft carrier, like any large warship, was organized somewhat like a small city. The commanding officer, the captain, was in complete command and had full responsibility for the operation and internal administration of the ship, for its safety and all aboard it, and for the performance of its mission. He was assisted by a second in command, the executive officer. Various departments were responsible for particular functions: the engineering department operated and maintained the propulsion machinery; a communications department was responsible for operating and maintaining all visual, radio, and radar communications equipment; the hull department was in charge of mechanical services such as damage control, a fire department, and carpentry shop; a supply department took care of food services, pay records, laundry, post office, and barber shop; and a medical department had doctors, corpsmen, and a small sick bay with an operating room and a few recovery bunks.

Unlike a city, an aircraft carrier had two departments for performing its war mission: an air department and a gunnery department. The air department operated the ship's aircraft; maintained, armed, and fueled them; and operated the catapults and arresting gear on the flight deck. A large number of pilots, air crewmen, plane handlers, mechanics, armorers, and ship's officers were required by this department.

The gunnery department, the group I was in, was responsible for operating and maintaining the ship's antiaircraft guns. The *Cowpens* had 26 40mm guns, in six quad groups and one pair; and about 15 20mm guns. The 40mms were small cannons, the projectiles of which were 40 millimeters in diameter and about five inches long. The cartridge that would propel the attached projectile to an effective range of almost a mile was approximately 20 inches long. The cartridges, or shells, came in clips of four with the bases of the shells attached to a brass base. The clip was dropped into a slot in the top of the gun, and as the gun fired, successive clips were fed by hand into the slots. Each gun fired at a rate of about one shell a second. The cannons were called "pom-pom" guns after the sound made by one gun, firing alone. Since the guns were mounted in groups of four, and there were three groups on each side of the ship, I can't remember hearing a single gun firing. It was usually all the guns on the port or starboard side of the ship firing at once: either at a target sleeve pulled by a plane in practice, or at attacking Japanese planes.

The 20mm guns were like large machine guns. Bullet and cartridge was about eight inches long with the base of the cartridge being about an inch in diameter and the base of the bullet 20mm. The cartridges were in circular drums that were attached to the side of the gun. The rapidly firing 20mms were aimed by a man strapped to a shoulder harness at the rear of the gun. The circular cartridge drums were replaced manually

Author's gunnery division in front of *Cowpens*'s island. Author is second from right. Chief Boatswain's Mate Ellsworth is at extreme right. Junior officers are at left. Ship's bridge is at left end of island, above the bull. Signal bridge, telescope are at right end of island. (Official Navy photo, 1944.)

when exhausted. The 40mms were aimed by a gunner in a tub to the side of the gun mount. When the gunner aimed his electrical, gyroscopic sight at a target, the gun mount turned and the gun barrels were elevated electrically in alignment with the sight. Every fourth projectile, 40mm or 20mm, had tracer illumination in its base. The gunner could see the path of his projectiles and correct his angle of lead.

Each group of 40mms and pairs of 20mms were mounted in protrusions, or tubs, just below the flight deck level so that ammunition, stored in magazines under the flight deck, could supply them. The gun crews reached the tubs by ladders up in the sides of the hangar deck and passageways beneath the flight deck.

Upon my arrival on the *Cowpens* I was assigned as the second junior officer in the 2nd gunnery division. The division, of about 50 men, two junior officers, a senior division officer, and a chief petty officer, was charged with the operation of two or three of the 40mm quad mounts and some of the 20mms on the starboard quarter of the ship. The captain's motor whale boat, the "Captain's gig," was slung beneath the flight deck overhang in that area so the division had the care and maintenance of it as well as the living areas of the enlisted men.

Shipboard living arrangements operated by the theory that "familiarity breeds contempt" with an accompanying breakdown in discipline and efficiency. Chief petty officers slept and ate apart from enlisted men in their own compartments, with their own kitchen and mess. Officers lived in "officers' country" in the forward part of the ship with their own kitchen, wardroom mess, and heads. The captain was most isolated of all, with his own office, living quarters, mess, and orderlies. He had his own sea cabin, where he could eat and sleep when the ship was underway. The *Cowpens* sea cabin was two decks below the bridge, but even that wasn't sufficient for our first captain, as will be related later.

Officers from the gunnery department stood deck watches underway and in port in addition to their other duties. The officers-of-the-deck and junior OODs operated the ship when the captain was on or off the bridge. The OOD maneuvered the ship with orders to the helmsman for compass headings and the engine room for speed; saw that zigzag plans were followed; kept the ship in its assigned position in a task group with course and speed adjustments; sounded the general alarm, if necessary; took the ship out of the task group formation and into the wind for flight operations; sampled the crew's meal, (a tray was brought to the bridge if a mealtime occurred during the watch); and at the end of the watch, wrote the ship's log for that time period. The junior OOD assisted the OOD and was in training to be an OOD himself someday.

While the *Cowpens* finished its outfitting in the navy yard, our airgroup—planes, airmen, mechanics and maintenance people were at a naval airfield about 50 miles away at Willow Grove, Pennsylvania. Our landing signal officer, LSO, was quartered on the ship. The LSO was the flying officer who would stand on a platform on the port, rear corner of the flight deck and with hand and arm signals with colorful cloth "paddles" direct our pilots on their final landing approaches.

To collect their flight pay, which was ordinary pay plus one-half, flying officers attached to ship or other duty had to log four hours of flight time a month. One day as we ate lunch in the wardroom, our LSO told me he was flying over to Willow Grove, probably to log some flight time, and asked if I wanted to go along. I did, and after making arrangements to leave the ship we departed for the yard airstrip.

Our plane was an SNJ, a single-engined, advanced trainer. The SNJ was the Navy designation of the Army Air Corps advanced trainer, the AT-6. This was the plane they used by the dozens at Craig Field, in Selma, so I was familiar with them though I had never flown in one. They were low-winged monoplanes, had retractable wheels and two seats, in tandem, covered by a plastic canopy. We put on headphones and parachutes, as required, and strapped ourselves in, I in the rear seat if I remember correctly.

Airborne and clear of populated areas, probably over the New Jersey pine flats, my friend said on the intercom, "Let's do some aerobatics." I said, "Okay," as if I enjoyed some every day, and he began. I've never had such a ride, in anything, ever, and wouldn't want to again, ever. We rolled, looped, did what were called "Immelmanns," and flew upside down, hanging on our seatbelts.

I suppose he was a good pilot or I wouldn't be writing this, but twice I thought we were going to cash it in. We came out of one loop, heading for the trees at such an angle that I couldn't believe he could pull us out with wings on the plane. But he did, just over the treetops.

The other incident was on landing at the practice field. When we arrived, some of our airgroup planes were doing a bounce drill. An outline of the *Cowpens* flight deck was painted in white on the runway. Each pilot would make his powered approach as if to land, cut his power and drop the plane onto the aft section of the deck. When the plane bounced into the air, he would gun his engine and climb away for another trip around the landing pattern. My pilot got into the pattern with the intention of making a regular carrier approach land, but instead of bouncing off would remain on the ground, finish his landing run, and taxi to the parking area.

The standard landing procedure was for a pilot to fly along the starboard side of the carrier, about 200 feet above the water and on a parallel course with the ship. About a half mile ahead of the ship he would make a slow, 180 degree turn to his left, coming out of the turn about a mile from the carrier and on a reverse course from that of the ship. When the plane reached a point even with the carrier's stern, the pilot would start another 180 degree turn. In this final, banking turn the pilot had to watch his airspeed closely, since with his wings tilted they would lose lift, and with insufficient speed the plane would start to stall and slide off toward the lower wing and the water. When the pilot came out of this last turn, at just above stalling speed, he would see the landing signal officer on his platform. The LSO, with his hand paddles, would show the pilot the position of his wings and whether he was too high or too low, too fast or slow. When the plane reached the proper position over the deck, the LSO would give the cut throttle signal and the plane would drop its final 20 feet or so to the deck. The plane's tail hook would catch an arresting cable on the deck and it would come to a sudden, controlled stop.

Our problem was a lack of airspeed in that final turn. We were halfway into the turn, wings nicely banked, when the plane started to slide off toward the left wing and the ground. My pilot reacted quickly and in time. He leveled our wings, gunned our engine, and gaining speed, we climbed out of the landing pattern. Our next approach was a long, gliding one straight down the runway. Our return to Philadelphia was uneventful.

CHAPTER 4

Shakedown to Trinidad

THE *Cowpens* was soon ready for sea and we departed, on June 25th, on our shakedown cruise to Trinidad, British West Indies. Trinidad was the shakedown destination for the new carriers because of the Gulf of Paria. The island is the most southern of the Antilles island chain which loops east and south from Cuba to Venezuela. Between Trinidad and Venezuela is the large, almost land-locked Gulf of Paria. The Gulf has only two, easily guarded openings to the sea, making it perfect for carrier flight operations without danger from enemy submarines. It is approximately 80 miles long by 40 miles wide.

Our trip down the Delaware River and Delaware Bay was delightful. Just leaving the noise and smells of the Philadelphia Navy Yard would have been enough, but sliding past the green countryside on a fine day was almost too much contrast. The little towns and landings looked like scenic postcards.

As the river widened into the bay, the air freshened and even the ship seemed to change. The concept of a ship, the perception of it by those aboard it, changes miraculously when it leaves port. At a pier a ship might as well be an apartment building with a gangway link to the ordinary world. Underway it becomes an entity of its own, free to do as it pleases, to go where it pleases as directed by its crew, while sheltering its occupants from the hazards of the sea a few inches away. This new experience seemed to have two dimensions: the ship sheltered its crew and the crew had to manage the ship with some reason and orderliness. The tons of steel and machinery acquired a kind of personality.

Near Cape May we returned to the real world. We were joined by two destroyers and started on a zigzag course. German submarines were operating along the east coast, and for a U-boat to torpedo a brand new aircraft carrier on its maiden voyage would have been too much, from both our points of view.

When underway in the open sea, we followed zigzag plans. We had a book full of them with a number for each. Our destroyers took their stations a mile or two ahead of us, the guide ship, on true compass bearings from us. All the ships used the same numbered plan, turning the required number of degrees to port or starboard of the base course at the specified times.

Our little group traveled at no fewer than 20 knots or so. A successful torpedo attack would have to come from ahead of us. Because of the relatively slow speeds of submarine torpedoes, a shot fired from abeam or the rear quarter of the target, our ship, couldn't catch up with us if we were making a proper speed.

To protect us, and themselves, from frontal attack, the destroyers used their underwater sound gear, sonar, continuously. Sonar was an underwater detection device much like radar, except that it used underwater sound waves instead of atmospheric radio waves. The gear, in the bow of a destroyer, would send out an underwater signal that sounded like a high-pitched "pingggg." If the ping contacted a submarine the sound would be reflected to the operator's equipment. The gear could also hear sound from a submarine's propeller. At a contact, the destroyers would attack with depth charges, and we would take evasive action at high speed.

During our first days at sea the ship's operation was tested with speed and turn trials, and radars and other equipment were checked. Our airgroup flew aboard and began the practice which wouldn't end even after we reached combat in the Pacific. We were to dock at the Norfolk Navy Yard, and after a few days of loading spare aircraft parts, ammunition for gunnery practice, fuel, food, etc., we were to leave for Trinidad. Our Norfolk visit was longer than planned. We had our first mishap.

The entrance to Chesapeake Bay, between Cape Henry and Cape Charles, is 20 miles east of Norfolk. We entered the bay on a warm, calm, clear day. There was a high cloud cover. Without wind the bay was a sheet of gray glass. The ship channel, marked by red and black buoys, was approximately 400 feet wide. The buoys, 500 yards apart along the sides of the channel, made parallel lines for miles, until the most distant ones were lost to view. The buoyed edges of the channel angled across the enormous bay and led, eventually, to the entrance to the harbor at Hampton Roads.

The entrance was guarded by an under water net that stretched between Hampton, Virginia, on the north, to Norfolk on the south. The channel opening in the net was marked by two black, cylindrical drums, each almost 20 feet long by six feet in diameter. A moveable part of the cable, underwater net could be pulled across the opening to keep enemy submarines or torpedoes from entering the harbor.

We approached the net opening a little after 1200 hours, straight-up 12 noon. I had just come off a junior-OOD watch on the bridge and was watching our approach to the harbor with a few others on the flight deck. We were a couple of miles from the drum marking the right side of the entrance. The ship was headed directly for that marker. We continued straight for the starboard drum. Surely, we thought, whoever had the "con" (control) of the ship would ease our bow to port and we'd pass the drum to starboard. We learned later that the captain had the "con."

Our bow didn't move. The ship slid steadily down the right edge of the channel, the drum disappeared beneath our flight deck overhang, then clanked along our starboard side until it reached our starboard, outboard propeller. The steel cables of the net wrapped around the propeller like fishing line around an outboard motor. The dead weight of about half a mile of underwater net pulled the ship slightly to starboard and we stopped. We stayed there for three days until divers, sent from Norfolk with a barge tug cut us loose with acetylene torches. The ship was put into a navy yard dry dock; a new, shiny, bronze propeller arrived on its own railway flatcar from Philadelphia. The new propeller was installed and, finally, we were ready for our departure. A board of inquiry somehow found the captain blameless in the incident.

Our skipper, Captain Joe McGuire, U.S.N., not his real name, was beginning to establish himself as some kind of psycho. Other, more salty terms would fit him, but I won't use them here. He was a mustang, an officer from enlisted ranks; *Cowpens* was his first command and he was desperately afraid someone would do something to embarrass him and endanger his career. No one did anything to him; he made his own mistakes. He avoided blame, probably by shading the truth, and after he was transferred from the ship, in May 1944, we heard he had been promoted to rear admiral. It couldn't have happened to a sorrier, more ineffectual officer.

Despite the captain's strange mentality, the *Cowpens* developed into an excellent ship. Before we reached the Pacific the gun crews fired thousands of practice rounds and became efficient teams; the air group made hundreds of landings, takeoffs, and had hours of bombing and strafing practice on targets towed by the ship and planes. Engineers, communicators, technicians, and supply people learned their jobs and became familiar with their equipment. After a few combat operations, the ship became a finely honed machine; the crew knew their jobs and relaxed into them; *Cowpens* became a well-oiled unit. Morale was excellent despite the wart on our complexion: the captain. There were no regrets when he was replaced, routinely, in 1944.

In the meantime, I had to watch my step around the captain. Self-preservation demanded it. Junior officers who made obvious mistakes in his presence found themselves transferred ashore in places like Trinidad, Panama, or later, to remote atolls. Unfortunately I had to see a good bit of the captain. When underway, I had two-a-day watches on the bridge as a junior OOD. When we reached the Pacific and the war, I became the junior OOD at general quarters, battle stations. Fortunately, we had a sharp, Annapolis-trained Lieutenant Commander for the general quarters OOD. He was expert at doing his job while calming the captain when things became exciting.

Before we left Philadelphia, the word came down that the captain didn't like the sound of the word "cowpens." It sounded too bucolic, I suppose. We were told to pronounce it "cuppens," but the instruction didn't take and we were soon back to "cow pens," then the "Mighty Moo," and finally, the just plain "Moo."

After the Norfolk net incident, a new structure appeared on our open bridge. A metal bunk was welded to the outboard steel bulkhead. It was equipped with a metal frame to support a rubberized canvas roof and it had sliding side and end curtains for privacy and weather protection. The captain could remain on the bridge day and night to oversee the operation of his ship. He needn't go two decks below to his sea cabin, except to visit his head or take a shower. He didn't trust his OODs or junior OODs and the feelings were mutual. I wasn't afraid of him. I didn't think he was really crazy, but I was uneasy in his presence because of his strange, psychological quality.

When we were operating in the Pacific with the task forces, we had the incident that really tore it with me and the captain. We had high-frequency radio voice communication between the bridges of the ships. It was called TBS, talk between ships, and was used for direct, oral orders from the flagship to all ships in the task group. We were receiving some instruction on the bridge loudspeaker. The voice coming from the speaker had a rarified, pseudo-English, affected accent. After listening for a while the captain said, to nobody in particular: "Listen to that Harvard sonofabitch."

I was thinking along the same lines, but not as a *Harvard* s.o.b. I had heard humorous cracks at Harvard before, like those aimed at the government or the Internal Revenue Service. I would come up with a retort depending on the college background or status of my verbal sparring partner. But this guy was serious. There was no humor in his voice, and he was a Captain and I was an Ensign. I would let the remark go by. To my dismay, my senior division officer, a lieutenant with some s.o.b. characteristics of his own, who happened to be the OOD said, "Don't be so hard on Havud men captain, Mr. Sommers is a Havud man." I could say nothing. I was outnumbered and outranked. A smart remark would have been suicide. With, I hoped, no indication of anything unusual I stepped to the port pelorus and took a bearing on the guide ship until my murderous thoughts subsided.

After leaving Norfolk and Chesapeake Bay, we turned south, our destroyers birddogging ahead. Off the Virginia coast we turned into the

Torpedo planes over a CVL, possibly *Cowpens*. Notice the plane-guard destroyer at right of photo, and other ships of task group in right rear. (U.S. Navy photo.)

wind, took our planes aboard, and headed south for Trinidad. Some kind of drill was scheduled every day. Fighters and Douglas SBD dive bombers would be launched. The ship would tow a spar target a few hundred yards astern and the planes would attack it with their machine guns and practice bombs. The TBFs, in addition to flying antisubmarine patrols, would practice on the same targets and would tow a cloth sleeve target for the F6Fs to shoot at in the air. At times the tow plane would pull a sleeve past the ship for the ship's guns to practice.

The ship's 40 and 20mm guns had effective ranges of about half a mile. The ships we would operate with: the larger carriers, battleships, cruisers, and destroyers would do longer range antiaircraft work with their five-inch guns. Our best antiaircraft defense was, of course, our own fighters. In combat areas, each task group kept a combat air patrol, a CAP, aloft during daylight hours. The CAPs, from different carriers in the group at different times, were usually of four to eight planes, in groups of two, which could be directed by voice radio when enemy planes appeared on our radar scopes. Our relatively small guns were for close-in, last minute defense. What they lacked in range they made up in volume—they could fire large numbers of projectiles rapidly.

For air operations: launching or landing planes, an aircraft carrier would turn its bow into the wind. The faster the wind flow across a plane's wing the greater its lift and the faster it could lift off the ground or deck. On landing, a plane flying into the wind is able to land at a slower ground speed than if going downwind. For any air operation carriers achieved, with the ship's speed adjustments, about 30 knots of wind down the flight deck.

The carriers launched planes by takeoff runs or with a catapult. The latter had a hook which ran in a slot in the flight deck. The slot began about 150 feet from the forward edge of the deck. The steel hook, about six inches high, was connected by a series of pulleys to a steam-driven piston housed below. A plane to be catapulted would be attached, with

Torpedo planes prepare to land on *Cowpens*. Tailhooks are extended, but flaps have not been lowered. Torpedo planes had crews of three: the pilot at front of canopy; turret gunner in ball turret at rear of canopy; and belly gunner at rear of bomb bay. Note machine gun barrel at bottom of plane forward of tail hook. (U.S. Navy photo.)

a droppable cable bridle, to the hook. The tail of the plane would be held by a quick-release hook. Pull would be exerted by the forward hook. The pilot would open his throttle until his propeller was turning at takeoff speed and pitch; the launch signal would be given; the steam cylinder would be fired; and the plane would hurtle off the end of the deck at flying speed.

To operate, launch, land, maintain, and use the planes efficiently required practice. To operate the ship, its guns, and equipment required practice. Which is what the ship did daily—on our shakedown cruise, on our trip through the Panama Canal, until we reached Pearl Harbor in September 1943, and later when out of combat zones. The payoff, in combat, was in successful operations and lives saved—our lives.

One day in the Gulf of Paria it was determined that the surface radar needed calibrating. To adjust the radar a target would be needed and one of the ship's two motor whale boats would make an ideal target. My gunnery division was responsible for the operation and maintenance of the captain's gig. One officer would go with and be in charge of the whale boat. Since I was the junior officer in the division my selection was automatic. I was nominated and named; there was no election. We would be launched early the next morning.

The boat was kept in a sling, far aft starboard, under the flight deck overhang. Shortly after daylight six of us climbed into the boat. As the only officer aboard, I was in charge—my first and only command. I had an engineer to run the engine; two boatswain's mates for line handling; a helmsman for the rudder; and a signalman, with blinker light gun and semaphore flags to communicate with the ship.

When all was ready the sling was removed, the ship stopped, and we were lowered, by two cables attached to an electric winch, the long way down to the water. I had been told to take the boat about half a mile off the starboard beam of the ship, stop the engine, and drift while the ship circled us, calibrating the radar. The ship made slow circles around us, a mile or two away, for about half an hour. Then a blinker message began from the ship. We were not to get underway, but were to drift where we were. The ship would pick us up later. We acknowledged receipt of the order; the "F" (Fox) flag, for flight operations, went up on the ship's yardarm; and off it went, over the horizon, launching planes.

We were alone in our little cockleshell. Nothing was in sight to the north, east or west. To the south, the mountains of Venezuela were low, blue shadows on the horizon. The sea had about a two-foot chop. The sky was cloudless, and as the sun got higher it got hotter and hotter. There was enough wind to keep the sea, and the boat, bouncing, but not enough to cool us off as we drifted with the wind. There was absolutely nothing to do. We tried to get comfortable, get as covered as possible from the sun, and think about how not to get seasick.

Hours crept by. Now and then one of our planes would bank low, past us. The pilot would wave, we'd wave and off he'd go over the horizon. At least we weren't forgotten, and, presumably, the ship would return, sometime, to pick us up. Sea lore had it that if you looked at something fixed, like the horizon or the distant mountains, you wouldn't get seasick. It didn't work. One by one the men threw up over the side. Finally there were only two of us left: a bosun's mate and me.

It was about 11 am by then, the sun frying us from almost directly overhead. The bosun's mate and I decided to try the ultimate seasick preventer: eating. The theory is that what's going down can't come up. We opened the lunch, and that theory was shot down, or up, too. Some culinary genius in the galley had packed us a dozen Western (rigid, scrambled egg and ham) sandwiches, on light white, liberally slathered with catsup. They were, of course, stone cold. One look and we joined the infirm.

The rest of the day was a scene from the movie *Lifeboat,* without Tallulah Bankhead. We lolled in the sharply pitching boat the remainder of the afternoon, a plane checking by every now and then. The ship picked us up about dark. When they helped us off at the hangar deck level, I could hardly walk. The deck seemed to be pitching like the whale boat. We were back to normal by the next morning.

After about two weeks in the Gulf, with the ship anchoring at night off Port-of-Spain, we returned to the Philadelphia Navy Yard. Before we entered Delaware Bay, our planes were flown ashore, not to return until we reached San Diego a few weeks later. The *Cowpens* received mechanical work found necessary during the shakedown. Spare parts, fuel, bombs, ammo, and supplies for our trip to Hawaii were loaded. After a few days we left for Panama and the Pacific.

CHAPTER 5

Through the Canal to Hawaii

THE trip from Philadelphia to Colon, at the northern end of the Panama Canal, took about a week. On our arrival, a wooden platform about 12 feet high was lifted aboard and secured in the center of the flight deck forward of the island. The platform was equipped with a transit, similar to those used by surveyors, for use by a pilot to keep the center line of the ship in the center of the locks. A phone line from the platform went to the bridge and to lock engines, which running on tracks on the lock edges, would pull the ship through the locks. In the wider canal cuts, or Gatun Lake, when the ship was underway under its own power and rudder, the pilot could give engine and rudder instructions to the OOD. On the night of September 2, 1943, *Cowpens* anchored in Gatun Lake.[5]

The hull of the *Cowpens* had a foot or two of clearance between it and the walls of the locks, but our flight deck overhung their edges. Larger carriers had preceded us through the locks, so all the lamp posts along them had been removed. We were told that *Essex*-class carriers and battleships, whose widths were limited by the width of the locks, were barely able to scrape through. Indeed, the concrete lock walls were scratched and scarred.

Like all first-time visitors to the canal, we were impressed by the fact that the canal runs from northwest to southeast, and that the northern end, at Colon, is west of the southern end, at Panama City. Our transit seemed strange: a large, seagoing ship moving through a tropical jungle. The deep cuts through the mountainous country were impressive engineering achievements.

After leaving Panama it took about a week to reach San Diego, the extra time resulting from a roundabout, zigzag course to avoid submarines. The convergence of sea routes to the ends of the canal made happy hunting grounds for enemy submarines, so extra precautions were taken in those areas.

I had a pleasant incident in San Diego. We arrived on September 11, spent the nights of the 11th and 12th at a Naval Air Station pier, and departed on the 13th.[6] I had liberty and spent the last night at the Coronado Beach Hotel where a lot of partying was going on. Early the next morning I went out to the street in front of the hotel hoping to catch a ride back to the air station and ship. I was standing there looking expectant, thumbing would have been undignified, when a car stopped and the passenger door was opened by an armful of gold braid. It was the admiral in command of the air station. "Going to the air station, son?" he asked. "Yes, SIR!" I said, getting into the car. He asked me if I were attached to the *Cowpens,* knew, of course, all about where we had been and where we were going, and we had a pleasant conversation all the way to the station. He even drove me to the ship's gangway. When I thanked him and started to get out, he said "I sure wish I could swap places with you." I told him that if he could arrange it, I would be willing.

Our planes, which had been flown across the country, plus a few extras in transit to Pearl, were loaded aboard by dock cranes. We cast off for Hawaii and Pearl Harbor. All the way out, which took another week or so, the ship and airgroup had more gunnery practice.

Pearl Harbor and Honolulu are on the south side of the island of Oahu. We approached from the southeast, in the early morning of a clear day. A number of off-watch people were on the breezy flight deck looking for the landfall. A low grey line appeared on the northwest horizon and rose higher above it. It was Oahu. When the ship was about 10 miles offshore I could make out, at the base of the now green island, a pink hyphen, the Royal Hawaiian Hotel. To its right was a smaller, white dot, the Moana Hotel. Those were the only landmarks on Waikiki Beach, which is now covered with high rise buildings. As we came closer I spotted the Aloha Tower at the downtown harbor, And from near the entrance to Pearl Harbor, the profile of Diamond Head stood up like a cameo.

Pearl Harbor is west of Honolulu and is entered by a narrow channel a few hundred yards long. Sliding through the channel, to our right, we could look directly down the runway of Hickam Army Air Field. The airport was in use, but evidence of the 1941 attack was still visible. The steel frames of several burned out hangars and piles of debris could still be seen.

Inside the entrance channel, the harbor opens into what could be more accurately called a large bay than a harbor. In the center of the bay is Ford Island, large enough to accommodate an airstrip, hangars, maintenance shops, dry-dock, ship repair facilities, and around the island's edges, piers large enough for a number of large ships. Off the northwest end of Ford Island was an area large enough to anchor ships if all the piers were occupied. On the mainland, on the east edge of the harbor, were the submarine docks with their tenders and repair facilities. On the east side, what seemed to be a large pipe protruded out of what I remember as oily water. It was all that could be seen of the battleship *Arizona,* sunk with hundreds of its crew on December 7, 1941.

Pearl Harbor, in September 1943, was the main base for the naval war in the Pacific. It had facilities for docking, supplying, and repairing the largest ships which, like the *Cowpens,* were arriving from the States. As the headquarters of Admiral Chester Nimitz, the CINCPAC, the Commander-in-Chief, Pacific Fleet, it was the command center for all Pacific naval and Marine operations. All our submarine war patrols were based at Pearl. The submarines used alternate crews. While one crew took a "boat" on patrol, for perhaps six weeks off Japan, or in the China Sea, or off New Guinea, the other crew would be billeted for rest and recreation in the Royal Hawaiian Hotel, which the Navy had obtained for the purpose. The Marines had facilities at Ewa, west of Pearl; there were Navy airfields at Barber's Point and at Kaneohe Bay, on the north side of Oahu; the Army Air Corps operated from Hickam and Wheeler Fields; and the Army had a large post at Schofield Barracks. With the buildup of men, equipment, and supplies that were pouring in from the U.S., the island could have fought a pretty good war all by itself, and in fact, was doing so.

The *Cowpens* had arrived at Pearl on September 19th and we departed on the 29th for our first combat operation, a raid on Wake Island.[7] But before we left, I had a duty to perform. Two of my closest childhood friends, next door neighbors, and boys of exactly my age, already had been killed in the war. Emile "Snitchy" Siegel, a cousin of my Harvard friend, had been in training as an Air Corps bombardier in Texas. On his last training mission, a night flight, the plane spun in and the crew perished. The nickname, "Snitchy," resulted from his small size and hyperactivity; he was into everything. Maurice "Brother" Bloch, a new Army second lieutenant, had been on his way to combat in the Solomon Islands. He had been stationed at Schofield Barracks. His outfit had been on a night practice maneuver, and, returning to base, he and others had climbed aboard a tank for the ride back. The tank ran off a road, rolled down an embankment, and he was killed. He was buried in the Schofield cemetery. I had to visit his grave.

A bus took me, endlessly, through miles of pineapple fields, to the high, northwestern part of Oahu where the Barracks were located. I finally reached a building, at the edge of the cemetery, where the records were kept. I had never seen a military cemetery before and the sight was disturbing. Hundreds of acres of open, rolling terrain were covered by thousands of small white crosses, with here and there a six-pointed star.

As children in Selma, my friends and I, "Brother" and "Snitchy" among them, had ridden our bikes on the sandy, tree-shaded lanes through the local cemetery. Live Oak Cemetery was a normal, natural, peaceful place. The Confederate monument, the World War I cannons, and the American Legion flagholders marking veterans graves were familiar sights. The monuments were of all sizes and shapes, determined, I suppose, by the economies of the times, the accomplishments of the dead, and the wealth and desires of their survivors. They were memorials for people, my ancestors included, who had lived out their lives doing what they did, and who died, early or late, as a normal part of living.

The Schofield cemetery was anything but normal. Beneath those lines of white markers were the remains of thousands of young men, like me, who had been wrenched from their normal lives by world events thousands of miles away. Thoughts of mortality crossed my mind; the kind we all have at funerals or memorial services. How did they die? When? Where? Will I be there? Or where? When? How? Questions unanswerable and best unasked.

With directions of area, section, subsection, and row, I found my friend's marker in the treeless expanse. On my return to the ship, I wrote a long letter to his father.

Before leaving Pearl Harbor that first time, the Navy had one more training session for us. A fire on a ship at sea is a sailor's number one worry. An aircraft carrier, with thousands of gallons of high-octane aviation gasoline aboard, planes filled with it, magazines filled with bombs, ammunition, and torpedoes was a potential bomb itself. The Navy would teach us to extinguish fires quickly.

The firefighting school was in an open area containing a four-story, concrete building, one or two rooms deep, with floors and stairways (ladders) of steel gratings inside. Nearby were the charred remains of a few airplanes. We began with the aircraft fuselages. They were doused with oil and gasoline and ignited. In groups of three or four, officers in regular khakis, men in dungarees and long-sleeved shirts, we approached with hoses. One hose had a nozzle that threw a cone of spray about 10 feet in diameter over the entire area. The spray was surprisingly good insulation from the heat of the fire. The spray team could approach to about 15 feet from the fire. The other team, protected from the heat, would bring up a hose dispensing foam. The foam would cover the fuselage, and the fire, lacking oxygen, would be snuffed out.

Practicing inside the building was a bit scarier. An oil fire would be ignited inside the basement of the building, with smoke coming from all the doors. The inside fire simulated a fire in a compartment on a ship. A spray team would approach the door, and protected by the spray, enter the building. The other team would play a stream of water at the fire. The water would turn to steam and the confined steam would smother the fire. The spray allowed enough air behind it for the firefighters.

The next step was learning to use rescue breathing equipment. A rubber mask, with eye goggles, was strapped on our faces. Air bottles on our backs supplied the masks. With the equipment in place a man could go inside the smoke-filled building and drag out a weighted bag, representing a casualty. The graduation piece de resistance was a jump off an upper level of the building into a net. It sounds worse than it was. The net was like a large trampoline, maybe 12 feet in diameter, and held by six men. The jumper pushed off, stuck his legs in front of him, and landed on the back of his legs and seat on the trampoline.

The course paid off later. All carriers had crashes and fires on the flight or hangar decks. Fire equipment was strategically located, and the trained deck crews could extinguish the fires quickly. I never had to fight a fire, accidental ones or from enemy action, but knowing how to use the equipment, if it became necessary, was reassuring.

CHAPTER 6

Action at Last

AN October raid on Wake Island was our first operation. It sounded as if it might be a final training operation, a "milk run," against a real but lightly defended Japanese base. Wake is about 2,000 miles west of Hawaii, and was probably supplied from the big enemy base at Truk, a thousand miles southwest of it.

Our task group included *Cowpens,* two *Essex*-class carriers,[8] a few cruisers or battleships for antiaircraft defense, all in a circular pattern around the admiral's guide ship. An antisubmarine screen of 10 or 12 destroyers was deployed in an arc a couple of miles ahead. This was the basic unit used by the attack, fast carrier task forces for the remainder of the war. A task *force* consisted of two or more task *groups*. The ships within the task groups could be changed, depending on the availability of individual ships; and the groups could be deployed separately, depending on the tactical requirements of a strategic situation. The system, which I suppose evolved as the war proceeded, gave Admiral Nimitz and his commanders great flexibility in their prosecution of the war. Only one task group went on this raid, which turned out to be more than a milk run.

Our uniforms for combat were what we wore routinely, with a few additions. Officers wore their usual khaki, long-sleeved shirts and pants and soft, pointed "overseas" caps. Enlisted men wore their usual blue, dungaree pants, long-sleeved blue workshirts and their regular white, round caps. At sea, everybody wore a short, sheath knife on their belts. They were to cut lines if one became entangled and had to get loose in a hurry. They were kept sharp enough to shave with if you ran out of razor blades and had a steady hand. Before our first operation all hands were told to take a shower and to wear clean clothing to reduce infection in

Task group, in column, entering Ulithi Atoll, 1944. First ship is a CVL; next is *Essex*-class carrier, followed by three battleships. (U.S. Navy photo.)

case of puncture wounds. The bottoms of our pants were tucked into the tops of our socks and gloves were worn to protect against flash burns. A signaling mirror was put in a pocket to reflect the sun toward a search plane if needed for rescue from the water. A steel helmet, a gas mask, and life preserver were additions. They were kept in storage boxes near our battle stations. The helmets offered more protection than the cloth caps; the gas masks could have been left in World War I. After a few operations the gas masks and life preservers remained, unofficially but permanently, in their storage lockers. Ships' officers were issued .45 caliber, automatic pistols. For a couple of operations they were worn on web canvas belts, with extra clips of ammunition, around our waists. They were heavy, hot and useless, and were soon left in our individual lockers in our cabins.

On the morning of our first air strikes, the ship went to general quarters, battle stations, well before daylight. My battle station was on the bridge, as junior OOD. Pilots were in their cockpits and engines were warmed up in the dark. Bombs and machine gun ammunition had been loaded well in advance. When the time came to launch planes, the dark was turning barest gray and there was a light, morning mist blowing down the deck. The first planes were to be flown, not catapulted, from the ship.

The first plane, a torpedo bomber, trundled down the deck, its propeller tip throwing a cylinder of mist encircling its fuselage. It picked up speed and lifted off into the darkness, its running lights on so its followers could find it. Our antiaircraft guns, in their tubs around the flight deck were manned, their helmeted crews at battle stations on the gun mounts. After the first few planes took off, we, on the bridge turned our attention to our duties of keeping station on the guide ship, since, for this launch, the entire group turned into the wind so all carriers could launch for the first strike.

Suddenly the crash alarm went off. One of our pilots on his takeoff run down the deck lost his sense of direction and the plane went over the port side, through a 40mm gun mount, and into the water. After a shocked interval it was reported that eight Marines manning the gun and the second lieutenant in charge had been killed by the plane's propeller. I don't remember if the plane's crew was picked up. In a few minutes the takeoffs continued. After the strike was airborne on the way to the target and no "bogies," enemy planes, on the radar, the ship went to a lower degree of readiness.

Later that morning, at about 1000 or 1100 hours, we went to general quarters again. Enemy planes had been picked up on the radar, approaching the task group from starboard.

Suddenly an *Essex*-class carrier, about a mile off our starboard beam, opened up with its five-inch guns. Eight or 10 dark puffs of smoke from exploding shells appeared about 2,000 feet above the ship. In a few seconds I heard the sound of the guns; then a plume of gray smoke from a burning plane arced into the sea. More flashes from the carrier's guns, a few more dark puffs and another plane went into the water. It was unbelievably quick and over. No more puffs; no more planes. The task group moved, unconcernedly, over the sparkling sea.

***Lexington* pictured from *Cowpens* during task group attack in the Marshall Islands, December 4, 1943. *Cowpens* guns, in foreground, are 40 mm. Gray puffs are five-inch anti-aircraft shell bursts. White smoke, to left of *Lexington*, is exploding enemy plane which has been hit. (National Archives photo.)**

It was hard to believe what I had just seen. That those Jap pilots were trying to kill us, and we had killed them first; quickly, efficiently, without so much as a "how-de-doo." It was a scene from a newsreel and soon I would go out of the theater into the real world. But this was the real world and what I had seen had happened. I'll never forget the unreality, the disbelief, my detachment from that moment. I was acting a part unrelated to anything I had ever imagined or over which I had any control. But it felt exactly right that I should be there: on my ship, in my tin hat, doing what I had been trained to do; a cog in an awesome killing machine; thankful that we were doing the killing and not the other way around. The strange moment passed, lost among other, immediate events. The detached, fatalistic feeling returned many times later in the war, but never with the intensity of that first time off Wake Island.

Our burials at sea the next day were from a hangar deck opening, starboard side, forward. The bodies, sewn in new, weighted canvas bags, each under a flag, were lined up on individual plank platforms supported by saw horses. The chaplain read the funeral service; there may have been a hymn. As "Taps" sounded, the platforms were tilted, one by one, and the bags slid into the passing, sparkling sea. The flags, unsupported, flattened against the planks. This event, too, was quick, final, and moving.

I didn't know any of the enlisted Marines who died, but I did know the second lieutenant. He was a fellow junior officer in the wardroom. He was a stocky, pleasant, blond fellow from Washington state, named McKay. He had come from the University of Washington where he had played football. He had been married shortly before being sent to the *Cowpens.*

No wartime death is easy to rationalize, I suppose, but these seemed particularly unnecessary because they resulted from somebody's dumb decisions. I will never know why we had to launch planes before daybreak, when surprise, on a practice raid on a weakly defended island, didn't seem necessary. The bad timing may have been caused by local weather conditions unforeseen when the operation was scheduled a few weeks before, but the result was tragic.

Manning all antiaircraft guns, even those on the edge of the flight deck, was standard procedure at battle stations; but before daylight, when no enemy planes were in the area, and when the crews couldn't have seen one if there were, seemed particularly hidebound. That sounded like a local, *Cowpens* procedural decision; going by the book with no thought of unusual conditions. Errors of judgment in an endeavor as unusual as a war were commonplace. These were particularly shocking.

Somebody did learn from the incident. I don't remember men on gun mounts again during flight operations with no enemy planes in the area. They were nearby, but where they could take cover if necessary. I can't recall another pre-daylight launch, except for catapulting night fighters especially trained for their jobs.

We left Pearl for the Wake Island raid on September 29, 1943, and returned on October, 14th.[9] A few days later we went out again for a few nights to qualify night fighter pilots.[10] Somebody, somewhere had the idea that during night air attacks a couple of airborne fighters, tracked with radar and directed as usual by voice radio from a ship's combat information center (CIC), could be useful. They were, later, very useful. We had several night qualification sessions and normal flight operations and gunnery practice during daylight hours.

Flying from and landing on a carrier in daylight was dangerous enough, but doing it in the dark was extremely risky business. The pilots who did it volunteered for the duty and liked doing it. One of them told me that he preferred it because he didn't have to fly at all in the daytime.

The procedure went something like this: only two or three planes would be catapulted at a time by a task group. The pilots would, of

course, go on instruments immediately, climb and follow voice-radio directions from the ship. The ship's combat information center officer, or fighter director, would track the planes on radar and give them courses, speeds, and altitudes to bring them above and behind enemy planes. Our pilot would see the enemy's exhaust (our planes had no airborne radar), aim at it, and fire his wing guns.

Later in the war, I saw one of our night fighters do his thing. I suppose the talker from the CIC gave the bridge the word that one of our planes was closing in on a bogey at about 280 degrees, relative to the ship.

Opposite: *Cowpens* landing signal officer watches fighter (number 12) bounce over arresting wires and sail toward planes parked on forward end of deck. Above: The plane comes to rest among parked fighters. The plane just ahead of 12 had its fuselage severed completely by 12's propeller, just behind the pilot who had not climbed out of his cockpit. Miraculously, there were only a few scratches among deck crewmen. Several planes, beyond repair, were jettisoned. (U.S. Navy photos.)

Torpedo plane crashes on *Cowpens* flight deck. Deck crew has folded right wing preparatory to clearing deck so plane in background can land. Crewman in right foreground with cross on white helmet is a medical corpsman. Deck crewmen ("airedales") wear darker, cloth helmets. (U.S. Navy photo.)

We looked off toward the port beam about 30 degrees above the horizon. It was a clear night. Pretty soon, what looked like a three-inch line of light appeared: our guy's tracers. The line of light disappeared and an orange flame appeared where the line had ended. The flame enlarged, arced into the sea, and that was that.

A big problem for night fighter pilots was vertigo. A pilot on instruments might think that his instruments, which said he was flying straight and level, were wrong and that he was really in a banking turn. He might fly by feel, "by the seat of his pants," disregard the instruments, and thinking he was correcting to straight and level, actually get into a banking turn. With no visible horizon or outside reference point, he would eventually fly into the water.

The landing procedure also was tricky. To land, the pilot would turn on his running lights and get into a normal landing pattern. The blacked-out ship had foot-wide landing lights mounted flush with and near the edges of the flight deck. The lights had covers which were opened enough so that a slit of light came from each one. The slits were visible only from astern. The landing signal officer, on his platform on the aft-port corner of the flight deck, was dressed in fluorescent, reflective clothing of blaze orange and yellow. He held "paddles" in each hand containing strips of the same material. When the plane made its approach, a bright light would be turned on the LSO, making him look like an animated jewel coaxing an invisible bug out of the darkness. When the pilot got his "cut" signal from the LSO, he would drop his plane into the blackness between the deck lights, hopefully to catch an arresting wire.

Should the pilot not get his plane into the proper attitude and position for landing, the LSO would give him a "wave off" (arms crossing each other rapidly overhead), the pilot would pour on his power, pull up in a bank to his left, and go around for another attempt. If he was descending too fast to pull out he would go into the drink. The plane guard destroyer would pick him up if he could get out of the plane before it sank. The pilots, night and day, really earned their pay.

After midnight, on our second or third night out, well south of Oahu, we had another mishap. I had been on the bridge on a routine 2000 to 2400 JOOD watch. The watch had been relieved and I was below, sound asleep in my bunk. At about 0200 the general alarm went off, a sound on the speaker system that would wake the dead. It sounded like someone with a heavy hammer beating measuredly and loudly, on a suspended section of railroad rail: "CLANNNK"; "CLANNNK"; "CLANNNK"; "CLANNNK." I jumped into my pants and shoes, and buttoning my shirt, headed for the bridge. How could we be attacked so close to Pearl? It had to be a submarine.

On the bridge I got the word. One of our destroyers had plowed into our starboard quarter. I had felt nothing. We had gone to general quarters to "button up" the ship; to close all watertight doors to isolate the damage and prevent flooding of adjacent compartments. Whenever

Bow of *Abbott*, DD 629, in Pearl Harbor after collision with *Cowpens*, October 1943. Several men asleep in bow of destroyer were killed. (U.S. Navy photo.)

a carrier had flight operations, a destroyer would take a "plane guard" position astern to be in a position to pick up flyers if a plane went into the water. The destroyer, *USS Abbot,* DD-629,[11] had been ahead of us off our starboard bow, in antisubmarine position. When the time came to take his position astern, the OOD evidently decided to slow his ship, let us go by, and then make a turn to his port to get behind us. He turned too soon; we didn't get past him; and his bow went straight into our starboard quarter.

We were lucky. The *Abbot*'s bow went into our chief petty officers' galley. Below the galley, and our waterline, were a few decks of store-rooms. Immediately fore and aft of the galley were chiefs' and enlisted living compartments. Had *Abbot*'s bow gone into us 10 feet either way we would have had scores of casualties.

The *Abbot* wasn't so fortunate. The velocity and weight of our ship smashed about 30 feet of the destroyer's bow into a complete, right angle. Several men, asleep in their bunks in *Abbot's* bow never knew what hit them. Another costly error of judgment.

We returned to Pearl and a dry-dock for repairs, and were lucky again. A dry-dock is like a long, U-shaped slip cut into the earth beside a harbor. The open end of the "U" has two, large, hinged, watertight gates. When ready to receive a ship, the water level inside the dock is the same as that of the harbor. The dock gates are opened, and the ship is positioned in the center of the dock and moored firmly in place. The gates are closed, the water inside the dock is pumped out, and the ship settles onto large, precisely positioned blocks to support its keel and hull. There it would sit, held by its inertia until, repairs made, the dock was refilled, and the ship floated again.

While our repairs were being made, which took about two weeks, the captain, wasting no time, had the ship's crew down in the dry-dock chipping barnacles and rust off the hull and painting on zinc chromate, rust-preventing paint. Concrete steps, built into the sides of the dock, allowed us to reach the bottom. Platforms rigged with pulleys high on the hull allowed the men to work on the skin of the ship. The junior officers and chiefs of the working divisions went into the dock with the enlisted men and supervised the work.

Being on the floor of a dry-dock with a ship towering over you was quite an experience, one I had at Norfolk and never expected to have again. The centerline of the ship's bottom, the keel, rested on dozens of laminated, wooden blocks, each about four feet high by six feet long by four feet wide. Other taller blocks were positioned on each side of the keel to support the hull and keep the ship from rolling over. Each class of ship had its own block plan, so the blocks could be positioned to fit a particular hull. On a cross-section of the hull from the keel to where the hull curved up to vertical was about 35 feet. I could walk under the ship, toward the keel, for about 15 feet before my head would touch the hull.

Actual overall length of the *Cowpens'* hull was 623 feet; its hull width was 71.5 feet at its widest point; and its flight deck was 109 feet wide. To look straight up for 80 or 90 feet to the overhang of the flight deck was

***Cowpens* in Pearl drydock after collision with *Abbott*. Men on platforms are unenthusiastically chipping rust and barnacles from and applying rust-preventative paint to hull. Khaki-clad officer, with overseas cap, on right of photo looking up at hull, may be author. (U.S. Navy photo.)**

an impressive sight. Every surface was slightly curved, horizontally and vertically. The ship weighed about 13,000 tons, calculated by the weight of the water displaced by the hull. Below the waterline, which is most of what you see from beneath a ship, the welded, smooth steel plates of the hull were a very dark gray, almost black. They were mottled with lighter, greener spots where marine growths and barnacles were attached, and orange spots of rust.

For some engineering reason, the bottom of the bow of a large ship has a bulb-shaped protrusion extending about five feet forward of the vertical reach of the bow. Near the stern, four bronze propellers, two on each side of the hull, were attached to shafts in housings faired into the bottom of the hull. Each propeller must have been about 12 feet in diameter. Aft of the last two propellers hung the huge, hinged rudder. Had the ship rolled off its blocks, the men in the dock would have been like ants under an elephant.

While our crewmen were chipping barnacles and yard workmen were repairing the gash in our hull, we had a fire in the dry-dock. I wasn't in the dock at the time, but I was on the ship. Somebody aboard, thinking he was draining a ballast tank of water, turned the wrong valve and drained hundreds of gallons of aviation gasoline into the dry-dock. Most of it got into one of the large drains in the floor of the dock. When it ignited, a tongue of flame, higher than the flight deck, erupted from the drain. We pulled out all our hoses on the hangar deck, the Pearl fire trucks arrived, the fire was extinguished, and nobody was hurt. All the men in the dry-dock were far enough from the fire to escape injury. The only damage to the ship was the black streak left by the flames going up the hull.

Before our collision, the *Cowpens* had been scheduled to go with a task group in an attack on Rabaul, the big Japanese base on the eastern end of New Guinea. *USS Monterey,* CVL-26, took our place. The task group took a pretty good shellacking by land-based planes and several ships, including *Monterey,* were damaged and had a number of casualties.

We started to think that the Moo was a lucky ship, if the luck would hold. It did, as it happened, through about 40 air attacks until the end of the war.

CHAPTER 7

Island Hopping Westward

THE basic strategy for the war in the Pacific was island hopping. Admiral Nimitz, from Pearl, was in command of the Navy and Marine forces, operating mostly across the central Pacific; General MacArthur, starting from Australia, directed the Army and Army Air Forces northward and westward up the Solomons, New Guinea, and the Philippines. The separate or combined forces would attack and secure an island or base, as was done in the Solomons; replace their losses, and attack and invade another island. The next target would not, necessarily, be the next geographically adjacent, Japanese base. Two or three might be skipped and the fourth invaded, leaving those passed to "wither on the vine."[12]

An example of a Japanese base skipped and left to wither was Truk. This large base, on an atoll in the Caroline Islands, was heavily defended and was the keystone of their defense of the central Pacific. It was the Japanese Pearl Harbor, their main anchorage, supply and staging base. Nobody really wanted to mess around with Truk. Our carrier groups worked it over several times, usually on our way to or from some other operation. Each attack would stir up clouds of AA fire against our planes and swarms of their aircraft to attack our ships. But Truk was never invaded; the cost would have been immense and unnecessary. After our invasions of the Gilberts and Marshall Islands in the central Pacific, Truk was skipped and the next invasions were in the Mariana Islands at Saipan, Guam, and the Palaus; and at Hollandia in western New Guinea.

Cowpens first invasion operation was in the Gilbert Islands in November 1943. The main landings were on Tarawa and were extremely costly to the Marine landing forces. The operation was typical of many to follow. A huge armada of warships, troop transports, supply ships and landing craft would land several Marine and/or Army amphibious divisions to invade and secure the target island or islands.

The fast carrier forces would establish complete air superiority over the landing beaches and destroy any ground installations in the immediate area. After a few days, as the ground fighting continued, we would go a few hundred miles to hit the nearest Japanese base to prevent any reinforcement, by air or otherwise, of the invaded island. A fleet of escort carriers, older warships, and Air Corps planes from nearby bases would continue to support the invasion until the operation was completed. This was the general scenario for the invasions of the Gilberts, Marshalls, Marianas, New Guinea, the Philippines, Iwo Jima, Okinawa—the *Cowpens* was in all of them—and finally, strikes on Japan in preparation for what was expected to be the most difficult invasion of them all. We were spared that ordeal by the atom bombs and the end of the war.

The *Cowpens,* in the Gilberts operation, left Pearl with two new *Essex*-class carriers, the *Yorktown* and *Lexington*. The former ships bearing those names had been sunk in 1942. We were accompanied for AA and surface protection by three new battleships, *Washington, South*

***Cowpens* refueling at sea from "oiler" *USS Platte*, AO24. Oilers also supplied aviation gasoline.**

Dakota, and *Alabama;* and about a dozen destroyers for an antisubmarine screen and their five-inch AA protection. This group, Task Group 50.1, was one of several attack and support naval groups involved in the operation.[13]

Until we left Pearl, only the captain and a few senior officers knew where we were going. Soon after we cleared Oahu, the captain came on the speaker system and announced where we were heading and what we were going to do. A copy of the op plan, (operations plan), appeared on a wardroom table. The plan was a bound stack of mimeographed sheets (there were no photocopiers then) about two inches thick describing every detail of the operation from the day we left our bases until we returned. Task group numbers, ships, support groups, invasion beaches and the divisions to land, embarkation and landing times, and for the carriers: plane types, bomb loads, numbers of planes in strikes and CAPs (combat air patrols), times of takeoffs, etc. I wondered who planned, wrote, organized, collated, and distributed this monumental mass of paperwork.[14] Amazingly, the operations went off pretty much as set out in the op plans.

Since my battle station was on the bridge, and my curiosity would get me through our part of the op plan, I was able to understand and observe the operations of our task group. Personnel below decks, in damage control parties, on engineering watches, and "airedales" on the hangar deck were kept informed of what was happening topside, particularly daring enemy air attacks, by announcements on the speaker system. As junior OOD, I made some of the announcements. When our guns were firing, no announcements were needed.

We left Pearl for the Gilberts on November 9th and returned on December 8, 1943. We made air strikes on Mili, Makin, and Tarawa for a day or two before the Marines landed on Tarawa. While the Marines secured Tarawa in a ghastly operation, our task group went north to the Marshall Islands to attack bases on Kwajalein atoll to prevent enemy air interference in the Gilberts.[15]

On this sortie, *Cowpens* and task group had its first attack by possibly 20 or 30 enemy planes. The attacks began on the afternoon of December

4th and ended at about 0130 on December 5th. We remained at general quarters the entire time. From time to time, five or six planes would attack the group. They were land-based light bombers, Bettys mostly, which had evaded our combat air patrols or came out after dark when our CAPs were aboard. We were not using night fighters yet. The ships with radar-controlled, five inch guns, the big carriers, battleships, cruisers, and destroyers if in range, would open up with their long range guns, the sky filling with dark gray puffs. When a plane would get within range of our 40mms and 20mms, we would start firing at them.

One particular scene sticks in my memory. A single-engined Japanese plane headed directly for us, to starboard, about 100 feet above the water. He had been hit and was trailing a thin stream of dark smoke. He was trying to crash into us before going into the water. All of our starboard guns were firing at him, tracers going right by, and, it seemed, into him, but still he came, on and on. I was saying to myself for somebody to get him, get him, boy, somebody GET HIM! At last somebody did. A burst of flame and white smoke erupted from a wing root. The wing tore off, the plane came apart, and the flaming ball smashed into the water a hundred yards away.

Most of *Cowpens'* combat actions were similar to that one, without the splash coming so close. Since our guns had no radar control, we did little firing at night, unless there was a very bright moon. Our bigger brothers and sisters with radar put on the night fireworks displays. Again, a spectacular incident comes to mind. One dark night, with several bogies and lots of firing, we were steaming along at battle stations, unable to do anything but watch. (Somebody said that what we needed was a neon sign on the flight deck with an arrow and the words: "The BIG carriers are over there.") I heard a twin-engine plane fly directly over us from stern to bow. He must have been at three or four hundred feet and had not seen us. A battleship was half a mile ahead of us and had evidently been tracking the plane with its radar fire control directors. When the plane got over the battleship, streams of the ship's tracers converged. The plane exploded into a large orange ball which dropped into the black sea, burned a minute or two and went out.

This sequence of *Cowpens* photos of a plane landing while on fire appeared in *Life* magazine in the fall of 1944. Former Lt. (j.g.) A. W. Magee, the pilot, described the incident to the author at a *Cowpens* reunion in the 1980s. Magee said that shortly after takeoff he smelled gasoline strongly. He radioed for and received permission for an emergency landing. When he cut his throttle on final approach the fire broke out, but he didn't know it. He made a good landing,

catching an arresting wire (raised above deck), and as soon as his plane stopped, made a hasty exit along the wing. A deck crewman caught him when he jumped off the wing. Note parachute caught on edge of cockpit. Propeller had not stopped completely. Deck firefighters are already in action. Below, the happy end of Magee's close call. The fire is extinguished and activity on deck is returning to normal. (U.S. Navy photos.)

The war was an impersonal killing game. Kill him before he kills you. Get enough of his planes, ships, and bases and the war will be over and we can go home. Meanwhile we do what we're out here for and hope our luck holds out.

After eight or 10 air attacks, I began to wonder: Will *my* luck run out? After 18 or 20 attacks, I knew it would, sooner or later; probably sooner since I'd had so much good luck already. Then the question became: Will I get out of combat before it does? The Lord, or Fate, or Something had been kind so far. Maybe it would continue. But when my number came up it would, and there was nothing I could do to change the outcome.

What made me and others such fatalists were incidents like these: during one recovery of fighters with the ship at battle stations, we on the bridge heard a sharp "barrrrack." Then the noise stopped. A plane that had landed had been unhooked from his arresting wire and was starting to taxi to park on the forward end of the flight deck. The pilot had accidentally hit his firing switch and the circuit was still on. The "barrrrack" was the sound of his wing machine guns firing a few dozen rounds. Luckily the plane's nose was up, tail down in taxiing position. The plane was lined up straight with the flight deck. The bullets went harmlessly in the air, to the left of the island and angled over the planes and men forward. Had the plane been turned toward the island there would have been many casualties. Had the pilot hit the switch with his tail in the air after catching his wire, with the plane's guns pointed straight along the deck, numbers of casualties could have occurred among pilots parking planes, deck crews, and plane handlers working on parked planes. No one was hit.

Another, more eerie, incident: we were at anchor, between operations, in one of the atoll lagoons. Some sailors were shooting basketballs on the forward elevator, which was down at hangar deck level. When the elevator was down it had passed and tripped electric switches which raised steel guard railings around the elevator opening on the flight deck. When the elevator went up it tripped the switches and the railings retracted into the flight deck. There was a separate switch for each section of guard rail. A sailor was sitting on the flight deck, his legs dangling over the edge of the opening. He was holding on to one of the stanchions supporting that section of rail, watching the play. The basketball bounced high on the wall of the elevator shaft, hit the particular switch of the particular section the boy was sitting under; the rail section came down and the sailor was killed.

One of the most active years for the *Cowpens*[16] was 1944. In January we struck, with other task groups, Eniwetok and Kwajalein atolls in the Marshall Islands invasion. February saw raids on Truk; a night attack on us off Ponape, another night session off Saipan; and attacks on Saipan, Tinian, and Guam in the Marianas, March found us hitting and being attacked near Palau, Yap, and Woleaie.

April saw the invasion of Hollandia in extreme western New Guinea, followed by other raids on Truk and Ponape in the Carolines on our way back to our base at Kwajalein in the Marshalls. On June 6th we departed for the Marianas. June 15 was D-day (disembarkation day) for the invasion of the Marianas. On June 12 and 13 our task groups hit bases on Saipan, Tinian, Guam, and Pagan Islands. On the 16th and 17th we had strikes on Iwo and Chichi Jima, in the Volcano Islands, the route of air reinforcements from Japan.

June 19 saw the Battle of the Philippine Sea, or "The Great Marianas Turkey Shoot" as it came to be known. The Japanese sent out a massive force of carriers, battleships, cruisers and destroyers to stop our invasion of the Marianas which would cut their sea routes to the Philippines and southward. Admiral Raymond Spruance, in command of the Fifth Fleet, had a larger force than the enemy. When the battle ended, between 300 and 400 enemy carrier planes had been shot down by our planes and three Japanese carriers had been sunk by our submarines.[17]

Other enemy carriers and ships were damaged. We, on our carriers in four task groups, saw none of the main action since it all occurred about 100 miles away, though we did have an occasional enemy air attack. Our combat information center, CIC, people could follow it on our radar screens and plots. At about dark, planes from the last strikes and dogfights started returning. Low on fuel and running out of daylight, they landed on the first carriers they found. Some didn't make it and ditched into the sea. Destroyers ran in all directions picking up wet airmen.

I remember one fighter pilot coming in with most of his rudder surface missing. With so little rudder control he could make only the most gradual of turns. He made a straight descent from several miles astern. He knew, and everybody topside on *Cowpens* knew, that the end of the approach would either be a normal landing, or a waveoff without much turn to port and a ditch in the drink since his fuel was insufficient for another long approach.

He landed his plane like a dragonfly on a lily pad. His gradual descent brought him over the end of our flight deck in perfect position. He got his cut signal, lifted his nose, and made a perfect three-point landing to catch an arresting wire. He didn't bounce. No tire screeched. There were about four inches of surface at the top and bottom of where his rudder had been.

When general quarters ended, I went by the CIC, combat information center, to "see" the air battle on the plotting screen. Our CIC room was a fairly large compartment, possibly 20 by 30 feet, located about amidships under the flight deck. In one corner of the room was a large, vertical panel of clear, thick plastic. The panel was about seven feet wide by seven feet high, with inscribed, concentric rings about a foot apart. A dot in the center, where a vertical and horizontal line intersected, represented our ship. The lines represented compass directions of north, east, south and west, with north at the top. The rings, depending on the scale selected, indicated miles from the center. The panel was lighted, indirectly, by bulbs around its edges making the etched, straight and circular lines gleam brightly white against the dark background behind the panel.

Two sailors behind the display, equipped with markers with luminous paint made small "X"s on the panel representing their and our aircraft: red for theirs and white for ours. Information for locating the "X"s came through headphones from men looking at radar consoles in other parts of the room.

Our airborne planes could be distinguished from theirs by an electronic device, IFF, identification-friend-or-foe, carried on our planes. The device made a distinctive mark on the radar "blips" of our planes. The concentric rings represented distances from the ship; the straight lines compass directions. The "X"s marked on the panel showed the locations of planes, theirs or ours, relative to our ship in the center. With the indirect illumination of the panel, the colored "X"s, and white lines and circles made a colorful representation of what was going on in the air up to a hundred miles from the ship.

At a table facing the screen, our fighter director officer, with radio voice communication to our planes, could give courses, speeds, and altitudes so our white "X"s could intercept their red "X"s on the panel. Every minute or so, after a few sweeps of our radar, the sailors behind the panel would update the locations of the varicolored "X"s. When the intercept was made, the pilot's voice on the speaker in the room would cry, "Tallyho!" followed by how many and what kind of enemy planes he could see. A minute or two later the report usually would come, "Smoked" or "Splashed" one or more Zekes [Zeros], Bettys, or Helens, as the cases might have been. Film from the planes' gun cameras would verify, later, the verbal radio reports.

After a usual intercept of a few enemy planes, the panel would show a string of red "X"s met by a line of white ones. Where the lines met would be a time notation, followed, usually, by the words "Splashed (how many whatevers)." After the "Turkey Shoot" the panel looked most unusual. On the upper left side of the panel was a foot-long smear of red at the end of lines of white "X"s coming from near the center of the panel.

Although the Japanese had several carriers remaining after the battle and some carrier planes, their losses of trained carrier pilots was catastrophic; their naval aviation capability had been shattered.

CHAPTER 8

Respite at Pearl

AS THE war and our task forces moved westward, our bases of operations moved too. After the Gilberts were taken, the fleet based in Majuro Atoll. After the Marshalls, we moved to Kwajalein and Eniwetok Atolls. Other bases were at Ulithi in the Marianas; Manus in the Admiralty Islands; Leyte, after the central Philippines were secured; and later, Buckner Bay, off Okinawa.

With the large number of warships, troop transports, landing craft, supply vessels, submarine tenders, oilers, floating dry-docks, etc., used in an invasion, it made logistic sense to send men, planes, repair facilities, and supplies to western bases rather than mount every operation from Oahu, so far to the east.

The atolls were ideal sites for naval supply bases. They were enclosed, continuous coral reefs surrounding deep lagoons, as much as 30 miles long by eight or 10 miles across. They were formed during millions of years as volcanic islands sank slowly into the sea. Coral reefs formed in shallow water along the edges of the original peaks. As the island slowly sank, the coral organisms, thriving in shallow, sunlit water, continued to build the reefs, vertically, to the ocean's surface. After thousands of years, with the original peaks hundreds of feet below the surface, the coral continued to build on their original foundations. Where floating material—palm leaves, coconuts, seaweed—caught in the reefs during thousands of years, islands formed like odd-sized beads on a string. Some of the islands were large enough for, first, native villages, later, Japanese installations, and, finally, U.S. naval bases and air strips. All of our naval units worldwide could have been anchored in many of the atolls, safe from submarines, with room to spare.

After the Marianas operations the *Cowpens* would not resupply and await the next operation in an atoll. We had been steaming for more than a year and needed a thorough navy yard overhaul. Our airgroup had been aboard since Philadelphia and was due for replacement. We left Eniwetok on July 8, 1944; departed Majuro on July 10th; and arrived in Pearl on the 16th. We didn't return to the war until the 10th of August.[18] As it happened, our respite in Pearl had some memorable moments.

At the first opportunity after docking on Ford Island, several of us continued a ritual we had developed on our returns from our sorties at sea. We headed for a hotel on Waikiki Beach for *fresh*, excellent food. A few blocks west of the Royal Hawaiian, right on the beach, was a small hotel named the Halekulani. After months of dehydrated potatoes, powdered milk, and canned beef stew, the cold fresh lettuce, pitchers of fresh milk, and filets, medium-rare, were fantasies to be fulfilled. If the Halekulani is still there, here's a toast to its dining room and its chefs of 50 years ago!

I don't remember any serious, shipboard duties, during that visit. The ship's personnel were given R and R, rest and recreation, while the ship was repaired, but some interesting incidents come to mind.

A pilot acquaintance needed to get his flight time. Did I want to fly with him to Hilo, on the big island, Hawaii, eat lunch, and fly back? I managed to work it into my busy schedule. We got a SNJ at the Ford Island strip and took off heading south. Again, I think I was in the rear seat. After clearing the island we turned left, east, past Honolulu, Waikiki, and Diamond Head. Off Koko Head we made a prescribed, 360-degree, counterclockwise turn for radar identification purposes, then headed southeasterly for Molokai and Maui. It was a fine, blue day and the dark green, mountainous islands rose sharply from the glistening sea. From our altitude of about 8,000 feet the islands looked deserted. There seemed to be few buildings; no roads or towns; just the green shapes with cliffs plunging hundreds of feet into white breakers.

Approaching Maui, my friend said on the intercom that we were going to fly into the Haleakala crater. Since he seemed to know what he was doing, I said, "Fine." He knew what he was doing and it was fine. The crater of the extinct volcano is, I suppose, about six miles long by a

Famous picture of carriers anchored in Ulithi Atoll, December 1944, in what was billed as the greatest array of sea power ever assembled. The central row of carriers were, from front, *Wasp*, *Yorktown*, *Hornet*, *Hancock*, and *Ticonderoga*. To their left, without camouflage, is *Lexington*. Among the CVLs pictured is *Cowpens*. White line across background is the atoll reef.

mile or two across. The entire top of the mountain must have blown off in some distant geologic age. The floor of the crater must have been a thousand feet below the rim. We crossed the crater's edge, descended a few hundred feet, and on each side of the plane the rim of the crater was a few hundred feet above us. We sailed along, straight and level, for a few minutes. Then our nose came up, the rim zipped below and behind us, and we were up in the bright sky again.

High above the sea, between Maui and Hawaii, my pilot asked me if I'd like to fly the plane for a while. I had never controlled a plane before, nor have I since, but my friend was in the plane, too, and it seemed a good time to try it. The green, aluminum joystick, with a black, rubber handle at the top, if I remember correctly, stood vertically between my knees. I took hold of it lightly, as I was told. I put the balls of my feet lightly on the rudder pedals. The throttle lever was on the left bulkhead of the cockpit, and I was not to fool with it.

When I was ready, my friend said, "OK, you've got it." He had told me to move the stick and rudder pedals gently. I pushed the stick forward. It wasn't gently enough and the nose dipped rapidly. I corrected quickly, too quickly, and we started to climb too fast. The nose went up and down, up and down, and then I discovered I was pushing the stick to the right and the right wing was somewhat down. We buck-and-winged around the sky for a while until I discovered that the plane would almost fly itself if I would let it. The slightest pressure on the stick, to right or left, would bank the wings; forward or back would raise or lower the plane's nose. A slight pressure on the left foot pedal, and the nose would go to the left; a little left pressure on the stick, with the left rudder, and we'd make a gradual, banking turn. At last I was able to follow our compass heading without too many gyrations. We were headed south-east toward the right, west edge of Hawaii.

We were flying at about 8,000 feet, and ahead to our left were two volcanic peaks, the top of each being higher than we were flying. The volcanoes must have been about 30 miles apart; Mauna Kea on the left and Mauna Loa on the right. My pilot told me to make a slow turn to the left and go between the mountains. The mountain to our left was much closer, and it must have been dry since the vegetation on it was more brown than the green we had left on Maui.

We were flying over the shoulder of Mauna Kea when something began to bother me. The altimeter read 8,000 feet, but the vegetation on the mountain's slope looked much closer. I could see individual, stunted trees. I told my friend my problem and he said he would take us on to Hilo. After landing I got the explanation: the altimeter was set to read from sea level; Ford Island was a few feet above sea level. The top of Mauna Kea was about 14,000 feet above sea level. The shoulder of the mountain, which we were above, was about 6,000 feet above sea level. The ground had been close; about 2,000 feet away. I had forgotten the sea level setting of the altimeter.

We took a taxi to the hotel downtown in Hilo and had a good lunch.

A sign in the lobby said that the Hilo Rotary Club was meeting there. We could hear them singing in a room nearby. On the way back to the airport, my friend stopped at a florist and had a lei of miniature orchids, packed in dry ice, airmailed to his wife, stateside.

On the return to Oahu, we passed low by the south side of Molokai. On a shelf of land above the sea, below the main plateau of the island, stood a group of white buildings. I was told on the intercom that they were the Molokai leper colony. The only other leper colony I had ever heard of, I think from a magazine article, was at Carrville, Louisiana. The cure for leprosy was one of the technological benefits of the war. A doctor friend told me that penicillin, an antibiotic first used during the war, wiped ancient leprosy, like other bacteria-caused diseases, from the list of world health scourges.

We made our identification turn off Koko Head, landed at Ford Island, and made it back to the ship in time for supper.

THE PRESIDENT, FDR, '04, sailed into Pearl to consult with his naval and military commanders.[19] U.S. presidents, in those days, did no overseas flying and very little domestic travel by air. When Mr. Roosevelt went abroad, to a meeting off Newfoundland with Churchill in early 1941, he went aboard the cruiser *Augusta*. On this trip to Hawaii he was aboard a newer cruiser, the *USS Baltimore*.

The ship had been fitted with a small elevator, so the president, a polio victim, could ride in his small wheelchair between decks. The day the *Baltimore* sailed into Pearl was a red-letter day.

To greet the commander-in-chief every ship was "dressed" with pennants on lines from bows, to mastheads, to sterns.

The rails of every ship and the flight decks of every carrier were manned with a sailor, in dress whites, every few feet. As the *Baltimore* slid along the west side of Ford Island waves of Navy, Marine and Air Corps planes swept overhead. During my three years of active duty, I wore my dress white uniform three times: for before and after the war photographs and this once, in 1944.

After the *Baltimore* was secure at its pier and the crews manning the

President Roosevelt, face obscured by general's riding crop, reviews troops during Oahu visit, 1944. Below, a tired president awaits a meeting, Pearl Harbor, 1944. (U.S. Navy photos.)

President Roosevelt (center), Admiral Nimitz (right, in white uniform), and General MacArthur (left in flight jacket) during photo session aboard *USS Baltimore*, Pearl Harbor, July 26, 1944. The first officer to the left of MacArthur is Admiral Leahy, the president's naval chief of staff, in Navy's new gray uniform. Note stack of helmets behind the president and MacArthur.

rails were dismissed, some friends and I, back in our usual khakis, headed for the officers' club. The club had a small patio behind it and at the rear of the patio was an eight-foot board fence. On the other side of the fence, and parallel to it, was a long, concrete pier. About a hundred yards down the pier the *Baltimore* was moored.

By pulling tables against the fence, and standing on them, we had a bird's-eye view of activity around the *Baltimore*'s gangway. The activity began with the arrival of high-ranking Army, Navy, Marine, and Air Force officers: the Navy in dress whites, the Marines in dress blues, the Army and Air Force in dress khakis. Braid shone and leather gleamed. In small groups they ascended a gangway to a wooden platform, then another gangway, at right angles to the first, to the *Baltimore*'s main deck.

Finally, after a long and dramatic wait, General MacArthur made his entrance. He got out of his car, surveyed the scene and allowed the scene to survey him, which we did, gathered his aides and scurried up the gangway. Unlike the other bigwigs, he wore no tie, had on his trademark crushed khaki cap and sunglasses, and wore a leather flight jacket. His only PR item not in evidence was his corncob pipe. He stood out from his fellows, as he always arranged it. He was truly a caricature of a caricature, but being the ranking officer and popular old hero that he was, he could get away with it.[20] The activity on the pier diminished; we returned to our tables leaving a lookout.

After half an hour or so, our lookout at the fence reported activity at the gangway and we returned to our observation posts. The president, it appeared, was about to leave the ship. A large loading crane was positioned near the gangway. The crane lifted a small, wooden platform, fitted with wooden side rails, to the main deck of the ship. A number of officers and sailors surrounded a seated person in their midst, and the knot of people got aboard the platform. When the signal was given, the crane operator (who must have been sweating blood) lifted the platform clear of the ship's deck; swung it smoothly out over the pier; and set the VIP load, ever so gently, beside an open, convertible limousine. The aides helped the president to the right rear seat in the car. When the order was given the car started slowly, flags flying from its front fenders, down the pier directly past our fence.

I wish I could say that the president, waving his cigarette holder, greeted us jauntily as he passed. I can't. We were shocked. The president of the United States, the most powerful leader of the free world, looked like a ghost. He was dressed in a white linen suit. His skin and hair, under a white Panama hat, was a grayer yellow than his clothing. Deep in the seat of the large car he looked neither right nor left, a tired, worn figure looking straight ahead, seemingly at nothing. The motorcade passed. He was dead within a year.

OUR YARD period over, *Cowpens* left Pearl on August 10th to rejoin the fleet at Eniwetok Atoll and, finally at long last, I was on the underway OOD watch list. After about five years of training for it, I was to be in charge of operating the ship, with oral orders to a helmsman, engine room talker, and junior OOD; underway, with full responsibility for its operation when the captain was off the bridge. At battle stations, an experienced OOD would take over, but during routine, task group steaming I was to stand OOD watches. It was a satisfying development.

Captain McGuire had been relieved by Captain Herbert Taylor, a relaxed, competent skipper who knew what was going on in all parts of the ship and let his officers run their affairs. When he was on the bridge, he said little but you knew your every move was being observed. If a correction was needed he let you know it, quietly. He trusted his officers and men and we trusted his ability and fairness. Morale soared. His first act was to have McGuire's bridge encampment removed.

Captain Taylor's hobby was target practice with a .22 caliber pistol. He had a .22 barrel and mechanism mounted on a .45 frame. On fine days during routine steaming, the captain would stand on the outboard wing of the bridge and shoot at flying fish when they were flushed by the ship's bow and sailed away far below. I don't believe he ever hit one, but when we heard the "pop, pop" of the skipper's pistol all was right with the world.

The ship reflected the new captain's attitude. As a relaxed, experienced team we were ready to rejoin our sister ships, help finish the endless war, and, finally, go home.

CHAPTER 9

Flanking the Philippines

AFTER the invasion of the Marianas, the next strategic objective was the western Caroline Islands, the Palaus, Yap, and Ulithi. Possession of Ulithi, Pelelieu, and Morotai, east of the southern Philippines, would give us staging areas for planes and ships for a Philippine invasion; cut Japanese supply routes from the south; and neutralize any Japanese airfields on Halmahera and New Guinea.

This operation was commanded by Admiral William "Bull" Halsey, Commander Third Fleet. The commands of the attack, fast carrier task forces alternated between Admiral Halsey and Admiral Spruance, the tactical genius of Midway. When Admiral Halsey was in command it was the Third Fleet, Task Force 38, Task Groups 38.1, 38.2, .3, .4. When Admiral Spruance was in charge, it was the Fifth Fleet, Task Force 58, Task Groups 58.1, .2, etc.[21]

Cowpens, with the new *Wasp* (CV-18) and *Hornet* (CV-12), *Belleau Wood* (CVL-24), three heavy cruisers and 11 destroyers, comprising Task Group 38.1, left Eniwetok on August 29,[22] for the area around the southern Philippine island of Mindanao. Strikes were flown over and around Mindanao including sweeps at the Cagayan area, Sarangani Bay, and one sweep over Zamboanga, where, according to the 1920s song, the monkeys have no tails.

Little Japanese resistance was found and the task group headed south for Morotai in the Molucca Islands, to support MacArthur's amphibious landings there.[23] Again little opposition was encountered, so our group went into the Celebes Sea with strikes on Menado, Celebes, and installations on northern Borneo.

Finding little resistance in the area south of Mindanao, 38.1 went north to join the rest of Task Force 38 off the central and northern Philippines. From the 20th to the 24th of September, the task group attacked targets around Manila on Luzon, and in the central Philippine area of the Visayan Sea, Cebu, and Leyte Islands. The group attracted several attacks by land-based enemy planes.

During our interruptive operations around the Philippines, the invasions of the Carolines proceeded. Pelelieu and Anguar, in the Palau Islands were taken and the atoll at Ulithi was occupied.[24] Ulithi was to become a major fleet anchorage and base for the remainder of the war. On September 28, after about a month at sea, 38.1 anchored in Seeadler Harbor, Manus Island, in the Bismarck Archipelago just north of New Guinea.

On October 4th orders were received by the *Cowpens* promoting several ensigns to the temporary rank of lieutenant (junior grade), USNR. My new rank dated from September 1, 1944. As I remember, my pay increased slightly; my duties remained the same.

MY *COWPENS* notes have a marginal entry that says we crossed the equator 12 times. This notation was made during the Hollandia, New Guinea, invasion, so I don't know what the grand total was. Each time we crossed, outside a combat area, an initiation ceremony was held by the "shellbacks," the old-timers who had crossed before, for the edification of the "pollywogs." I, of course, remember my initiation best. It occurred on our way to our first invasion, in the Gilberts.

Officer and enlisted pollywogs received the same treatment at the same time by officer and enlisted shellbacks. After getting new haircuts, delicately done with clippers, sometimes spelling out C-O-W-P-E-N-S in hair left on successive heads, we were taken to the flight deck where belt lines, without too many heavy blows, were run. My most memorable events were the garbage chute and the Royal Baby's Belly.

The former was a target sleeve, a light, nylon cylinder about 30 feet long, extended by aluminum rings, which was towed by a TBF for the ship and planes to shoot at. The sleeve was laid out on the flight deck and filled with buckets of wet garbage from the galley. We had to crawl through the cylinder, about three feet in diameter, while shellbacks whacked at our rears with their belts.

The Royal Baby's Belly was the climax. A fat, half-naked chief petty officer, with a gold, cardboard crown on his head, was seated on a "throne." He was assisted by a "court" of shellback attendants. The initiate was made to kneel in front of the chief's belly, which overhung his "diaper." The chief would take a handful of lubricating grease, from a drum at his side, slop it on his sweaty, greasy belly, and the pollywog would be told to "kiss the Royal Baby's Belly!" When the pollywog would hesitate, the chief would grab the back of his head and squish it into the gob of grease on his belly. I closed my mouth and eyes. I wish I could have held my nose.

We were presented later with the finest, most elaborate certificate that I own. It has a blue border embellished with fish, mermaids, and Imperium Neptuni Regis himself. It says in part, ". . . That on the 22 day of January 1944, in Latitude 000 and Longitude 178.57W there appeared within our Royal Domain the *USS Cowpens* bound south for the Equator and for Destination Unknown on mission of war . . . ," followed by my name in fine English script; that I had been initiated into the "Solemn Mysteries of the Ancient Order of the Deep"; and the signatures of Neptunus Rex, Ruler of the Raging Main, Davey Jones, His Majesty's Scribe, and the Commanding officer of the ship. The printed seal of the Navy Department, United States of America; and the embossed, gold seal of the *Cowpens* completed the production. Truly ". . . a thing of beauty and a joy forever."

ON OCTOBER 2 the task group headed north to attack Okinawa, in the Ryukyu Islands, and Formosa (now Taiwan) in preparation for the invasion of the Philippines at Leyte later in the month. Task Force 38 stirred a hornets' nest. On the night of the 12th, after a day of strikes on Formosa, we were treated to a night of air attacks. Since the *Cowpens* had no radar-controlled guns, we went to battle stations and watched the fireworks.

One night, after a day of strikes on Formosa, we had an attack at dusk. The cruiser *USS Canberra* was damaged. My notes say that 11 enemy planes were shot down, mostly by our CAP. The next night, the 14th, we were attacked again and the cruiser *Houston* caught a torpedo. *Cowpens*'s optical gunsights were usable in dusk attacks so we could do more than just watch the action. It is hard to remember particular actions, but those nights must have been pretty hot. My notes say that five-inch and 40mm tracers were zipping over us and other ships. Some may have been hit accidentally by our group's antiaircraft fire, but we were not.

The Japanese, trying to finish off our crippled ships, stepped up their air attacks. On the 15th, the *Cowpens* was detached from TG 38.1 and joined *Cabot* (CVL-28) to fly fighter cover over the damaged cruisers, now making about three knots, under tow southeasterly. We were accompanied by a few cruisers and eight or 10 destroyers for antisubmarine and antiaircraft protection.

We thought, at the time, that Admiral Halsey was baiting an attractive trap[25] for enemy surface units with the crippled cruisers, the two small carriers and the few cruisers and destroyers. His other task groups, loaded with *Essex*-class carriers, battleships and cruisers, operated north and east of us as our little group crept out of the danger area.

No enemy carriers or surface ships took the bait, and I don't know how many enemy planes were intercepted by the big boys, but our group really caught it—and the bait bit back.

My notes say that on the 15th some 60 Japanese planes were downed, mostly by our fighters; on the 16th *Cowpens* and *Cabot* planes got 41; and also on the 16th the *Houston* was hit by another aerial torpedo.[26] Both ships survived, made it back to the States, and were repaired.

During those extremely active days, the ship went into a special condition of readiness. I think it was called Condition A (or Able). When we weren't at general quarters all the ship's hands went to a watch-and-watch situation. Half the crew would go off battle stations to get a sandwich and sleep. Enough watertight doors would be opened to allow access to living areas. The other half of the crew would operate the ship

Task Group 38.3 entering Ulithi Atoll, December 12, 1944, after Phillipine strikes. From front, CVL *Langley*; *Ticonderoga*; battleships *Washington, North Carolina, South Dakota*; cruisers *Santa Fe, Biloxi, Mobile,* and *Oakland.* (U.S. Navy photo.)

and man half the guns. Flight operations occurred at scheduled times regardless of the ship's condition of readiness. Should bogeys appear on the radar, the general alarm would sound and the ship would return to general quarters, battle stations.

During one of our returns to battle stations, during this operation or another, an incident happened that I will never forget. The general alarm had gone off, in the daytime, and I was hurrying toward the island and the bridge. I came out of a passageway onto the starboard catwalk about 40 yards forward of the island. A four-step ladder led to the flight deck level where I was going. A TBF, back from an antisubmarine patrol, had just taxied and parked opposite the ladder landing at the flight deck. His wings had just been folded and I heard the whine of his bomb bay doors being opened. As I reached the flight deck level, the bomb bay opened enough for an "ash can," a depth charge, to drop loose on the deck. I took off for the island expecting to be flattened, at best, by a blast. Nothing happened, and safely inside an island doorway I realized why. Before a TBF attack on a submarine the depth charge fuses had to be armed, switched on, electrically by the pilot from his cockpit. They couldn't go off until armed to explode and then they wouldn't fire until they sank to a certain set depth when water pressure would trigger their fuses. Evidently the mechanism holding the depth charge in the plane's bomb bay had malfunctioned, and when the plane hit the deck in landing it had jarred loose. When I saw that depth charge clank out of that plane onto the deck, I wasn't thinking of explanations. I left there—*FAST!*

On October 20, with the crippled cruisers out of the danger area, *Cowpens* rejoined 38.1 and the group headed for Ulithi for refueling and rearming. Also on October 20, General MacArthur's invasion forces landed on Leyte Island in the central Philippines, supported by the Seventh Fleet.

The Japanese, determined to stop the invasion, sent most of their heavy surface ships in the south through the central Philippine seas to attack the invaders and sent their remaining carriers from Japan, with few planes, toward the northern islands to lure Halsey away from Leyte. The ensuing Battle of Leyte Gulf, a series of air and surface engagements, became the greatest defeat of the Japanese navy. Samuel Eliot Morison described it as ". . . the greatest naval battle of all time."[27]

CHAPTER 10

The Battle of Leyte Gulf

THE Japanese planned a desperate attempt to stop our landings on Leyte Island. They would send their largest ships—battleships, cruisers and some destroyers—eastward through the islands and seas of the central Philippines. A Japanese carrier group, from north of Luzon, would lure our Third Fleet away from the Leyte area while the heavy enemy ships went through the San Bernardino and Surigao straits, north and south of Leyte and Samar Islands. The surface ships would attack our Seventh Fleet, of old battleships, cruisers, escort carriers, transports, and landing craft, which was supporting the invasion forces.[28] On October 23 part of the enemy fleet was discovered by one of our submarines in the Sibuyan Sea of the central Philippines heading for San Bernardino Strait. The Japanese ships continued to approach the strait and were attacked by Task Force 38 planes. The enemy lost a few ships but several of their heavy ships got through the strait. On the 24th we lost the *Princeton*, CVL-23, to land-based planes from Luzon. The Japanese carrier group from the north was discovered and Admiral Halsey headed for it with task groups from TF 38 leaving the Seventh Fleet to defend itself, the ships in the Leyte Gulf, and the invasion area.

In the early hours of the 25th the classic battle of the war took place in Surigao Strait. To "Cross the T" was the textbook, winning tactic when surface fleets met. The last time it had happened was in the Battle of Jutland in World War I. In a grand mishmash of fouled communications, the German fleet had steamed in a column toward the British fleet. The British, in a rough column and on a course at an angle to the German one, crossed ahead of the German column.[29]

Heavy surface warships, battleships and cruisers, had two turrets of two or three cannons each, forward of their central, elevated fire-control towers. They usually had one turret aft. The British, crossing the top of the "T," had two enormous advantages. By training all three turrets of a ship toward the German column the British could fire three turrets to the Germans' two. The German ships couldn't fire their aft turrets because of the superstructures between their rear turrets and the British ships.

The other advantage for the crossing column came from the deployments of the opposing columns. The British, with all their firepower, could fire directly down the German column. If their shells missed long they might hit a ship beyond their point of aim; if short, a ship ahead. The German ships, with only two thirds of the firepower of the British, had to fire at a line of ships aligned horizontally to their lines of fire. If a shell fell long or short it was simply a miss; their targets were one ship deep.

The Battle of Jutland, in 1916, was the decisive, naval engagement of World War I. It marked the end of German surface naval power. That its tactics could ever be repeated, in an age of modern intelligence, communications, radar, and air warfare was unimaginable. The Battle of Surigao Strait saw the "T" crossed once more. The location of the islands determined the surface fleet deployments; the time of night, our destroyer torpedo attacks, and our radar-controlled guns determined the outcome.

The southern group of Japanese warships had to steam northward in a column through the narrow Surigao Strait between Leyte and Dinagat Islands, north of Mindanao. The time was about 0300 on the 25th so aircraft were not involved. Admiral Oldendorf, with the old battleships and cruisers of the Seventh Fleet, had his ships in a line across the mouth of the strait; a classic cross of the approaching Japanese column. When our radar showed the enemy in range, our ships opened fire. With the help of our destroyers and PT boats firing torpedoes from the flanks of the Japanese column, our old ships annihilated the enemy column. The ships that weren't sunk or run aground turned around to escape. Seventh Fleet escort carrier planes caught them at daylight.

Meanwhile, the Japanese cruisers and battleships that went through the northern San Bernardino Strait turned south and started to mop up with our escort carriers and destroyers off Samar Island. Several of our ships were sunk by enemy surface fire. For some reason, before sinking all of our escort carriers and destroyers, the Japanese commander turned away and headed back through San Bernardino to escape. Perhaps he received information that Task Force 38 was returning. It was. Halsey, with his battleships and cruisers, was hurrying southward to protect the Seventh Fleet.

My task group, 38.1, just back from its bait bit, was in Ulithi on the 24th for refueling and rearming when we were ordered to the Leyte area at full speed. It was an all-night, all-out effort. Thirty knots, or a little better, was all that the task group could make. Everything on the ship, as I recall, vibrated and rattled for about 14 hours. On the 25th, when we were about 300 miles from Samar we launched strikes which found some of the San Bernardino enemy units still in the area. Torpedo planes and fighters from Seventh Fleet carriers caught the Japanese cruiser *Mogami* in the Mindanao Sea and, after strafing it with rockets and machine gun fire, sank it with aerial torpedoes.[30]

Third Fleet carriers, minus 38.1, sank several ships of the Japanese northern force off Cape Engano of Luzon. The battles off and near Leyte Gulf were over. The Japanese fleet was no longer a threat. Task Force 38, which ". . . had been at sea, almost continuously for 84 days,"[31] retired to Ulithi for restocking, rest and recreation.

RECREATION in the atoll anchorages meant going ashore for the day, to an island beach with enormous dice games, lots of beer, and for the forehanded some whiskey. Before we left Philadelphia, a ships' officer whiskey pool was organized. We had loaded enormous quantities of beer for the enlisted men and CPOs beach excursions. The medical department had plenty of "medicinal" whiskey for the pilots after strikes. The ships' senior officers "anticipated" for the ships' company officers. Although bringing alcoholic beverages aboard U.S. Navy ships was strictly against Navy Regulations, the pool was set up with the full knowledge of the captain, executive officer, and all ships' company officers aboard. Each officer could buy a share for a cost commensurate with his rank; if you hadn't bought in you'd have been thought curiously square. Ensigns paid, as I recall, about $30.00. Lieutenant JGs $40.00, Lieutenants, $50.00; Lieutenant Commanders, $60.00, and on up to the captain who paid $100.00. Each shareholder was entitled to a few fifths of gin, bourbon, or scotch according to the quantities acquired. The whiskey was to be issued, one bottle at a time, only outside the U.S. where otherwise unavailable.

Somebody, it was said, knew somebody in the Schenley Corporation in New York. So one day six TBFs from our airgroup flew to New York, loaded their bomb bays with wooden cases of fifth-sized bottles, and returned to Philadelphia. That afternoon a block of wooden cases about 30 feet long by 8 feet wide by 5 feet high appeared on our hangar deck. It was guarded all night by armed Marines until it could be stowed in locked storage below. When we reached the atoll anchorages and the first bottles were issued most of us couldn't consume a whole fifth in one afternoon. We'd bring the remainder back aboard and lock it in our individual safes in our rooms. As far as I know, nobody drank when the ship was underway, but at anchor in an atoll, R and R required a snifter or two now and then. In combat areas, on special occasions, the alcohol regulation was honored more in being overlooked than in being observed.

The first constructions on a recreational island were said to have been an officers' club, CPO (chief petty officers') club, and an enlisted mens' club. Those were usually only roofed areas so the crap games and beer drinking were out of the sun.

Whenever I would arrive, as I recall, big dice games would be in progress. Many groups of dozens of officers would be around separate tables. The man with the dice would be covered for whatever he wanted to bet, and dozens of side bets went with every roll.

My childhood friends and I were taught to shoot craps by our African-American yard man, on rainy days, for pennies, nickels and dimes, when I was about 10 years old. He was an expert and he taught us well, but I could never make a dent in those atoll affairs. Since soap and cigarettes were the only things to spend money on, the men from the ships were loaded when they came ashore. Each roll of the dice saw a turnover of hundreds of dollars. I usually went ashore with $50 or $100, hoping to win $400 or $500 and then quit. I would sometimes get up to about $200 but the dice would get cold and, eventually, I'd lose my stake. Then I would go swimming, or to put it more accurately, looking at the underwater marine life.

In Honolulu I bought a swimmer's face mask. It was a rubber oval that fit across my forehead, around my temples, and under my nose. The front of it was heavy glass. With it in place, I could inhale a breath through my mouth, swim underwater and see clearly through the glass. When my breath was exhausted, I'd surface, take another breath and go down again. Snorkels hadn't been invented, so I had to surface for each breath. I didn't have to go deep to see the underwater sights. They were spectacular. The water was crystal clear. Big fans, domes, and branched bushes of coral were everywhere and in all colors. Schools of multicolored fish, unafraid unless I made a sudden motion, moved about. I wore a pair of canvas sneakers to protect my feet from the sharp coral, underwear shorts, and carried a spear to ward off dangers.

The spear was about five feet of heavy steel rod which someone in the ship's machine shop made for me by flattening the tip and sharpening it into a barb. I speared only one fish with it. A school of fish came by. I eased the barb close to a sizable fish and speared him. It was a total waste. I couldn't take him back to the ship and cook him and he wasn't so handsome wriggling on my spear. I kept the spear, though, in case some curious shark cruised by. I saw some small ones from a distance, but they left me alone and I returned the favor.

The British Navy had no anti-liquor regulation. In fact their naval tradition required the issuance of a daily ration of grog, a mix of rum and water, to all hands. Their officers received their rations in regular little bars near their wardrooms. They weren't limited to grog, either; they had normal bar bottles poured by a bartender. When anchored near a British ship, we arranged visits at cocktail time. When we reciprocated the visits, we would, privately, give them drinks in our cabins before taking them to the wardroom to eat. I have a dispatch, dated September 8, 1945, from a Sub Lt. Johnson, aboard the *Indefatigable*, a British carrier, thanking me, aboard the *Ticonderoga*, for my hospitality.[32] Our exchange of visits occurred in Tokyo Bay where we were anchored.

I have a vivid recollection of my visit aboard *Indefatigable*. I was taken to the flight deck to see where a kamikaze had crashed. The ship had an armored flight deck of steel about three inches thick. The plane had hit forward of the island, near the port edge of the deck, at a steep angle. There was a circular dent in the deck about 30 inches long by 16 inches across by about 4 inches in its deepest point. Lt. Johnson said that after the smoke and flame cleared away they just shoved what was left of the plane over the side. The big dent was the only damage.[33]

The flight decks on our carriers were about a half inch of steel overlaid with about three inches of wood, supported by steel I-beams underneath. The CVs had an armored hangar deck. The CVLs had no armor on the flight deck or hangar deck and only light, cruiser armor on the sides of the hull. When a kamikaze dove into our carriers they would go through to the hangar deck and explode. The resulting fires would take hours or days to extinguish. If they got out of control or into bomb or gasoline storage, the ship could be lost.

Not only were our drinking regulations different from the Limeys; our ideas of naval architecture were, too. We had some educational exchanges with our English allies, especially at cocktail time.

CHAPTER 11

My Last Run on the *Cowpens*

THE 1st of November, 1944, found *Cowpens* and Task Group 38.1 in Ulithi with Task Groups 38.3 and 38.4. Operations at Leyte were not progressing as planned. The Japanese were reinforcing their Luzon airfields and were sending convoys of fuel and supplies to support their land defenses. Task Force 38 was ordered to the Luzon area to disrupt the enemy supply efforts.

Task Group 38.1, now consisting of *Hornet*, CV-12, *Wasp*, CV-18, *Hancock*, CV-19, all *Essex*-class carriers; *Cowpens*, *Monterey*, CVL-26; six cruisers and 14 destroyers; and the other two task groups headed west. On November 5th our group began sweeps over the northern Philippines. Off Lingayen Gulf, on the west coast of Luzon, the group's planes found and destroyed a convoy of a dozen Japanese freighters, and for the next few days we attacked airfields near Manila.

The enemy was increasing the number of kamikaze, suicide plane, attacks. We enlarged the combat air patrols, CAPS, over our task groups from eight to 16 or more fighters, but on this operation the kamikazes were of little threat. Our main interests were with the weather and refueling and resupplying at sea.

Refueling and replenishing at sea were increasingly common operations. Two or three "oilers," small tankers, and supply ships carrying bombs, torpedoes and depth charges would meet a task group in need of replenishment.

For refueling, a warship would take a parallel course with and at the same speed as the oiler, about 30 yards to one side of it. Another ship would take a similar position on the other side of the oiler. Fuel hoses would be passed, by the tanker's cranes and booms, to the recipients. The ships would steam parallel while the fuel oil and gasoline were transferred. When the refueling ship finished its drink, the hoses would be retracted, the replenished ship would turn away and another ship would take its place. Bombs and ordnance were transferred in a similar way. The ordnance would be transferred by crane and cargo net from the supplier to the supplyee. With such supply the task groups could remain at sea as long as an operation required.

The officers-of-the-deck on the receiving ships had to be on their toes. The supply ships kept steady courses and speeds, but as anyone who has steered a boat knows: no waterborne craft travels in a straight line; its heading is corrected constantly. The receiving ships had to maintain their distances within fairly close limits. If a receiver moved too far away, the fuel hoses might break; too close and a collision had to be avoided. The entire group of ships traveled at about 18 knots, the speed of the tankers or supply ships. At times the seas were too rough to perform the operations, but most went off with a minimum of broken fuel hoses or lost supplies.

Transfers of mail and personnel were similar operations, but I will never forget one transfer of replacement pilots. My division had responsibility for the fantail, the curved, stern portion of the ship. As the division officer, I was in charge of the fantail operation which we had performed many times before.

Late one afternoon we were told a destroyer was coming alongside with mail and about eight replacement pilots. About 20 men from my division, my Chief Boatswain's Mate Ellsworth, and I gathered on the port side of the fantail.

The destroyer came up from astern, putting his bridge about even with our fantail and about 30 yards away. As he approached we shot a light line across his bow with a line-throwing gun. Sailors on the destroyer pulled in the light line with increasingly heavy lines attached until they pulled from us a line almost three inches in diameter. They attached their end of the hawser to a ring about eight feet above their maindeck. Our end of the hawser went through an overhead pulley, and the line was kept taut by about 10 of our men. As the ships separated, our men would let out on the line; when they converged our men pulled in

Members of *Ticonderoga*'s marine detachment are taken by bosun's chair to a ship that will take them to Japan for initial occupation duty, August 1945. The ship's company landing party, of which the author was a member, did not go. (U.S. Navy photo.)

the slack. A pulley that could be pulled between the ships was attached to the overhead line. Beneath the pulley a rope sling, or light cargo net, carried sea bags and mail between the ships.

The sea had a medium chop. The ships separated and converged and our men kept relieving and retrieving the supporting line as we took on bags of mail, official papers, and the pilots' personal bags. Occasionally the ships would close rapidly, our men couldn't take up the slack quickly enough and a bag of mail would bounce off a wave. It was getting dark and we hadn't taken a man aboard.

To pull men across on the supporting line, the cargo net was detached and a "bosun's chair" replaced it. This was a canvas bag with holes for a man's legs. Light lines attached it to the moving pulley above it. A man would be helped into the "chair" on the destroyer. Our men would pull the overhead line taut, and two of our men would pull on a small line attached to the pulley to pull the man across to our ship. We would help the man out of the "chair" and it would be returned to the destroyer for another passenger.

We had taken a few of the pilots aboard when darkness became a problem. The sun had set long ago and now we were running out of any light at all. Our high-line crew could barely see the angle of the hawser leaving our pulley, and was taking in and letting out the line by feel. All ships were blacked out at all times when underway, so any illumination was out of the question. The destroyer was a dark shape against a slightly lighter sky. The white coat of a steward's mate made a faint, gray spot on the destroyer. The bow wave of the destroyer and an occasional whitecap going by were the only light spots in a black-gray scene.

If our overhead line became too slack and we dragged a man into the water, his weight tangled in his seat and the speed of the ships might pull the overhead line from the control of our men. The possibility of drowning one of our charges was on all our minds. We had never made a transfer without seeing our lines, in total darkness, before.

I had a sound-powered phone line with a "talker" to our executive officer's talker on the bridge. Our executive officer was in charge of our ship's part of the operation. The executive officer would transmit his orders to his talker, a sailor with headphones and a mouthpiece; his talker would repeat them to my talker, who would tell them to me.

In my opinion, our operation in the darkness was becoming too dangerous to continue. I took the phone from my talker and told the exec's talker to put him on the phone. I told him my thoughts about continuing the operation and suggested it be finished in the morning. He told me, in language that won't bear repeating, to get the rest of those men aboard, NOW, and when he wanted my advice he would let me know. I said, "Aye, aye, sir!," and that was the end of that.

My men, my chief and I knew what we had to do. Without being able to see what we were doing, we had to keep the high line taut and pull some scared men across the dark abyss without drowning any of them.

Every man who could pull effectively, about a dozen of them, took hold of the high line. When the ships separated, a man would hold onto the line until it reached the pulley; he would release his grip and run to the rear of the group. When the line started to slacken, our men would haul it in, the last man on the line going to the pulley. It was a tug-of-war with our men pulling against a 2,200-ton destroyer. Nobody said anything. Everyone knew what he had to do and did it.

When we got the last pilot aboard, with only a few wet legs and bottoms, we couldn't have been more relieved. I was so proud of my men that I could have hugged them all, but that wasn't the thing to do. They knew, without my telling them, that they had done a great job, but I told them anyhow.

During this refueling and replenishing operation, the task group was carefully avoiding a typhoon that was passing the area. Typhoons, or hurricanes in our part of the world, were storms to be avoided. This one was the second to affect the *Cowpens.*

During our earlier typhoon, north of the Philippines, the force of the wind and height of the waves were unbelievable. A man couldn't go on any deck open to the weather. The few planes that couldn't be fitted into the hangar deck were well tied down on the flight deck. The ship rolled until one wondered if it would stop.

In the middle of one night we were awakened by the speaker system sounding general quarters. All watertight doors were closed and "dogged." The speakers announced, over and over, "The smoking lamp is out! The smoking lamp is out!" Two or three planes in the hangar deck had broken their tie-downs. With each roll of the ship they crashed about, like dice in a cup, destroying themselves and other planes around them. Hangar deck crews were trying to lasso and secure the hurtling chunks of metal. Heavy seas had bashed in some of the hangar deck doors and about a foot of seawater, topped with a few inches of gasoline from the sliding planes, sloshed back and forth. The ship reeked of gasoline. The least spark and we would have had an inferno. Thankfully, we didn't, and suffered only the loss of a few planes.

During *Cowpens*'s third, big typhoon, on December 8, 1944, I was on my way home. The ship had a fire on the flight deck. Several men, including the air officer, were swept overboard and lost. Seven planes, three jeeps, two tractor-tugs, and a mobile crane were blown from the flight deck. Three destroyers capsized and were lost. The task force lost 778 men and over 100 planes.[34]

The debacle almost cost Admiral Halsey his career. A board of inquiry investigated and the admiral was exonerated, barely.

On November 16th, I received orders sending me back to the States. On the 19th and 20th we had strikes near Manila and on northern Luzon. On the 24th, the task group anchored in Ulithi and I was detached. I boarded the *Enterprise*, CV-6, a passenger for the trip to Pearl.

CHAPTER 12

Back to the States

THE Bureau of Personnel dispatch from Washington ordering me and three other junior officers back to the States began, "FOLLOWING OFFICER DIRDET NOV OR DEC X PROCEED VIA FAGTRANS PORT US . . . ," which translated says "The following officers are directed detached in November or December. Proceed by first available government transportation to a port in the United States. . . ."

On our arrival in Ulithi, the first available government transportation heading east to Pearl Harbor happened to be the carrier *USS Enterprise*, CV-6. If I had been able to choose a ship for the trip, that is the one I would have chosen. It was the most illustrious carrier of the war.[35] On December 7, 1941, it had been approaching Pearl Harbor unaware of the attack. Some of its planes, attempting to land on Oahu, had been shot down. In 1942 it had flown CAPs for the *Hornet* when the Doolittle bombers were launched on the Tokyo raid. During the same year it had been in the Solomon's Islands battles, the Battle of Midway, and the Santa Cruz Islands battle. For a time in 1942, it was our only operating carrier in the Pacific. There were stories of it leaving Pearl with workmen aboard repairing it while it made appearances off Japanese bases so they would think we had several operational carriers.

Since the fall of 1943, when the *Cowpens* reached Pearl, we and *Enterprise* had been in the same operations, and we were, at times, in the same task groups. My college roommate, Jim Wolf, was aboard and I had visited it and him when we were anchored in the same atolls. The "Big E" was becoming a Navy legend, which would continue to grow through the remainder of the war. To have been aboard her for the trip to Oahu couldn't have been better luck.

I have a souvenir of that trip. It is a U.S. dollar bill with the word "Hawaii" printed in inch-high letters across the back, and the same word, vertically, on the ends of the front. Hawaii was then a U.S. territory, and the bills must have been especially printed for use in the islands. I had printed "Back to the States, *USS Enterprise,* Nov 24–Dec 6, 1944," on it, and there are about a dozen signatures, apparently of other friends and passengers. I can recognize the signatures of Jim Wolf and Ken Maudsley, Frank Brennan, and Alton Kayse, the other transferees from the *Cowpens.*

I can't remember much about the return to Pearl, but it must have been a delight: no duties, no watches, no general alarms, and no war; just relaxing with friends and fellow passengers and leaving the driving to the *Enterprise.*

After a few days in Pearl, the states-bound passengers boarded the *Matsonia* for the trip to San Francisco. The *Matsonia,* a former Matson Line cruise ship, was now a Navy transport. Before the war, she and her sisters, the *Lurline* and *Mariposa,* had taken tourists to Hawaii, Australia, New Zealand, and the orient. I can remember only two incidents on the *Matsonia* trip.

I had been assigned to a small, double cabin with a Marine captain. Each night of the trip several poker games took place in the ship's lounge area. I wasn't a poker player, so I didn't participate. The first night, my roommate got into a poker game. He was from Louisiana and told me his daddy had taught him poker when he was a child. He said the players in the games were a bunch of yahoos who thought they could play better than they could. He told me his wife was to meet him in San Francisco; he was going to win a few thousand dollars, enough for a few weeks at Lake Tahoe; and then stop playing. He did what he said he would do. After the fourth night he stopped playing. He had his money. Some of the players came by our cabin every night to try to get him back in the game ("Deal, cry the losers . . ."), but he wouldn't return. When the ship docked in San Francisco his wife met him on the pier; they waved goodbye and left for Lake Tahoe. I never saw him again; can't remember his name; but he must have been one helluva poker player!

The other incident was slightly troubling. One day, when a few of us were getting some sun and air on one of the ship's upper decks, we saw a Marine with a carbine slung over his shoulder looking over the rail at something below. We joined him to see what he was watching. On the deck below were about 40 Japanese prisoners-of-war. They had been brought topside, under guard, for sun and air. They were dressed, uniformly, in white tee shirts, white pants, and sneakers. They were short, had black, cropped hair, brown skin, and high cheekbones. They looked fit and happy as they smoked the cigarettes that had been given them. They should have been happy. They were alive and headed for a comfortable POW camp in the States for the rest of the war.

I had heard the stories of Jap atrocities: how they had decapitated captured pilots; machine-gunned downed airmen in the water or in parachutes; and the ghastly tales of the death march after our surrender on Bataan. Their fanaticism was well known: how they would play dead on battlefields and then jump up to kill as many of our men as possible before they were gunned down. On the invasion islands no quarter was given by either side. It was kill the Jap first, by any method, or he will surely kill you. In some of our island operations, no prisoners were taken. I don't question our GIs; under their circumstances I'm sure I would have done as they did.

In their air attacks on our task groups the killing was more impersonal. It was our machines against his machines; get his plane first before he bombs or crashes into our ship. Perhaps human feelings depend on personal situations. If I had seen friends killed by a kamikaze maybe I would have despised all Japanese forever. But I didn't and I don't.

Looking down on the prisoners, I, strangely, didn't hate them. My feelings were more of curiosity combined with distrust, a wariness, and awareness that, had our positions been reversed, we surely wouldn't have been on a weather deck of one of their transports enjoying the sun, air, and their cigarettes.

The physical differences between us were apparent; the other differences—backgrounds, cultures, educations, social, political, and economic—could be imagined. They seemed so different that I might have been looking at creatures from another planet. Differences between people and cultures can, I suppose, be resolved by time and contacts between men of goodwill. I didn't have the time, and certainly, then, neither the goodwill nor desire to understand the enemy and his mentality. I never saw them again.

The *Matsonia* arrived in San Francisco on December 18, 1944, and, according to the endorsement stamped on my orders, I reported to the Headquarters of the Twelfth Naval District for temporary duty pending further assignment by the Chief of Naval Personnel in Washington. While awaiting our orders, we were sent to the Mark Hopkins Hotel for housing. It was like throwing Br'er Rabbit into the briar patch, which may have been what the Navy intended.

For every serviceman in the Pacific, San Francisco was the object of his dreams. It was the United States again; it was the first stop on the way home; it was wine, women, and song; and the Top of the Mark was the symbol of it all. The Top of the Mark was the glass-walled cocktail lounge on the top floor of the Mark Hopkins Hotel. From it, then the highest point in San Francisco, the entire bay could be seen on a clear day. Every day, from about three in the afternoon when it opened, until about three or four in the morning, when it closed, the Top of the Mark contained one enormous 'rousing and carousing' party. Soldiers, sailors, marines, WACS, WAVES, and even female civilians met there for high old times. The Fairmont Hotel, across the street from the Mark Hopkins and also on the top of Nob Hill, had a USO (United Services Organization) service club, but it couldn't compare to the Top of the Mark. Other bars, like that at the St. Francis Hotel, near the bottom of the hill, also were in the comparative minor leagues. The Top was where the action was.

I checked every day, as instructed, at the Naval District to see if my orders had come in. They hadn't, worst luck, until December 22nd, so I had four days in Eden.

Being in the States again was a little strange at first. The *Cowpens* had been in war zones for about 15 months, much of the time in combat operations. We saw few civilians in Hawaii; there were naval or military people everywhere. On the ships, on the atolls and islands there were only men. So seeing well-dressed people, particularly civilian women, their high heels chattering on paved sidewalks, dodging auto traffic on busy streets among tall skyscrapers, was like being in a world I had almost forgotten. The women looked like models from *Vogue* fresh from Fifth Avenue.

I remember going to a cigar counter in the Mark Hopkins for some matches. (Cigarettes overseas were five cents a pack, untaxed, so I had plenty of those.) I saw some odd-looking Lucky Strike packages in the glass counter. The old Luckys had been in green packages. These were white. I asked the girl about the new colors. "Haven't you heard," she said, "Lucky Strike Green Has Gone to War." That was the new American Tobacco Company advertising slogan. Apparently everybody in the world had heard it but me.

While on the subject of cigarettes: the sailors on every ship were partial to their own particular brand. The *Cowpens* was a Camels ship. Everybody aboard seemed to smoke Camels. The ship's store sold Camels almost exclusively; nobody bought another brand. You couldn't give a carton of Luckys or Chesterfields away. My next ship, the *Ticonderoga*, was a Luckys ship. When I got to it, in about four months, I already knew that "Lucky Strike Green Had Gone to War."

One morning at about 3 a.m. (my orders had not yet arrived), I was walking alone up Powell Street toward the Mark Hopkins. I had just passed the St. Francis Hotel entrance and was at its upper, Post Street corner. There was no traffic on the streets and no pedestrians on the sidewalks. Through habit, I guess, I glanced around for traffic before crossing the street. I couldn't believe what I was seeing. Across Post Street, silently rolling down Powell directly at me was a car with no lights. Apparently it had slipped loose up the hill and was rolling directly at me at a good speed. I was in no danger; I had plenty of time to move out of the way. The empty car bounced over the curb, went between the hotel and a lamppost on the corner, and silently headed down the sidewalk toward the St. Francis entrance. The hotel had a striped marquee running from its doorway to the curb. I returned to my original spot, shouted to watch out below, and hoped no one would come out of the hotel at that moment. Nobody did. The car rolled, swiftly and quietly, under the marquee; its right front wheel banged into the far entrance of the building, apparently knocking both front wheels to the left. The car turned straight across Powell, went between two cars parked parallel on the other side of the street, and clunked head-on into the retaining wall of the Union Square park. There it stopped. There had been no sound, except for my shouts and the final clunks, during the entire incident. San Francisco had its perils, too, but my luck was still holding. I continued up the hill and went to bed.

My orders arrived on the 22nd. I was to report to the Commandant of the Washington, D.C., Navy Yard on the 26th of January, 1945, the delay to count as leave. On the 23rd I left, by commercial air, for Birmingham, via Los Angeles and Dallas. We were grounded in Dallas, for some reason, so I didn't reach Birmingham until the 24th. After standing up for most of the way on a crowded bus, I arrived in Selma after dark on Christmas Eve.

CHAPTER 13

Letdown at Home

AFTER all my anticipation of getting home, my time in Selma and later in Washington was a letdown, an anticlimax. The pace of events of the last 18 months; the new sights, sounds, and places; the exhilaration of riding the crest of the Pacific war was too much to turn off instantaneously. My mental tempo had to slow gradually, I suppose, and my four months in the States, while great, were not completely relaxing.

Selma or I had changed. It wasn't the place I had left. My mother had died in the spring of 1943, two months before I left for active duty. My father, very deaf and in his middle seventies, was in poor health but still lived in our home with a housekeeper. My brother, six years my senior, was in France with the Army. All the young men in my age bracket were somewhere in the armed forces; only a few of the girls in my age group were still around. Most had met and married aviation cadets in training at Craig Field, our local Air Corps base.

One friend, the late "Pookie" Tepper, was at home on leave from the Air Corps. He had been a bombardier with the 14th Air Force in China. Of the 15 or 20 crews he had left with, only two or three got back. He had changed. Before the war he had been a normally quiet young man. Now he couldn't stop talking—about anything, and was talkative for the rest of his life. He and I double-dated with a few of the girls left in town. The officers' clubs at Craig Field in Selma and at Maxwell Field in Montgomery, 50 miles away, were our only 'stomping grounds.' There was little to do in Selma and few people to do it with.

By this time in the war, everything in the civilian world seemed rationed. Ration boards in every county issued coupons to be used with money to buy gasoline and other essentials. Limited amounts of meat, sugar, and other groceries were available only with ration coupons. A note dated 12-30-44 on my orders from San Francisco said that I would be issued coupons for 10 gallons of gasoline, three pounds of sugar, 40 meat coupons, and 100 food coupons. The note was stamped: "War Price and Rationing Board, Selma, Alabama." I turned those over to my dad and his housekeeper, and having been given commissary privileges at Craig, supplied them with groceries from there.

The Air Corps was training French aviation cadets at Craig Field at that time. I recall walking down Broad Street, Selma's main drag, in my blue uniform, the standard Navy winter clothing. The French cadets had similar colored uniforms. A pleasant, elderly lady stopped me on the sidewalk and, thinking I was a cadet, asked me if I liked it over here. I said I sure did, but when the time came to report in Washington I was ready to go.

The Washington Navy Yard was on the Anacostia River just southeast of the Capitol. It had an airstrip; docks, one of which berthed the presidential yacht; and an ordnance and gunnery school which I had been ordered to attend. We lived in bachelor officers' quarters, BOQs, had meals in an officers' mess, and went to school in buildings on the base. The courses were technical explanations of the operations of the 40mm guns to which I had been assigned. I couldn't have cared less about learning the electrical and mechanical systems, but it was in Washington and we were free to go downtown when we weren't in class. For a while, unfortunately, my classes ran from 5 pm, 1700, to 1 am, 0100. While on that shift, I would go to sleep about 1:30, wake up about 9:30 and get downtown at about 11 am. Not much was happening that I was interested in, in the daytime, but I had contacts on the Hill.

Our Congressman, Samuel F. Hobbs, was from Selma; he, his wife and children were old acquaintances of my family, and his longtime, spinster secretary was an older friend. I would go to his office, ask Helen Goldsmith, his secretary, what was going on in the Capitol, and if anything of interest was scheduled she would give me tickets to the House or Senate galleries, or to a committee room. Occasionally Judge Hobbs would have me to lunch in the House dining room, or invite me to his home to dinner when I got on a more normal schedule. His wife was most hospitable. His children, two boys and a girl, were Navy officers elsewhere on active duty.

After I was aboard the *Ticonderoga*, my next ship, I was thumbing through *Esquire* and ran across a cartoon of two GIs in adjacent foxholes. Shells were exploding all around. One of the soldiers had a cute, blousy blonde on his lap. The other had a questioning look on his face. The caption read, "I just wrote my Congressman." I tore out the cartoon, wrote "When are these to be issued to the Navy?," and sent it, via Fleet Post Office, San Francisco, to Judge Hobbs. I received an answer in record time, in about three weeks. He said that when they were authorized for the Navy I would get the first one.

The night shift didn't last too long, and after a time my gunnery school friends and I got downtown after dark. So Washington wasn't a total social washout.

On March 31st I was detached from the Navy Yard and ordered to report to the Commandant, 13th Naval District, Seattle, Washington, for temporary duty pending first available transportation to the *USS Ticonderoga*, CV-14, an *Essex*-class carrier. I was authorized to delay until 20 April, 1945, in reporting at Seattle. When I reported as ordered, the *Ticonderoga* was across Puget Sound in the Bremerton Navy Yard. Again, I didn't have far to go.

The *USS Ticonderoga*, as she looked in Pacific battle readiness.

CHAPTER 14

USS Ticonderoga

THE *Ticonderoga* had been commissioned in early May 1944, and joined Task Forces 38 and 58 in early November, during the Philippine operations. On January 21, 1945, she was hit, in rapid succession, by two kamikazes off Formosa. One crashed into the top of the island, the location of many of the ship's gunnery officers. The ensuing explosion killed most of the gun control officers, the forward five-inch gun director was blown askew, the signal bridge was destroyed with most of those on it, and the ship's captain, on the bridge several decks below, was wounded. Anyone on or near the island structure was lucky to have escaped injury.

The other suicide plane crashed through the flight deck, slightly forward of the island, and exploded on the armored hangar deck. The resulting fire finally was contained and the ship was saved. She eventually reached the Bremerton Navy Yard where major repairs were made.

By April 1945, she was ready to go to sea again, and I was among the new crew aboard to take her out. We left Bremerton on April 21. Evidences of her damage were everywhere. Some that I particularly remember were in the shower stalls in the head (bathroom) that I used. Officers' country was forward of the No. 1 elevator, which was just forward of where the deck kamikaze had hit. The aft bulkhead (wall) of the head was the forward bulkhead of the elevator shaft. Four or five shower stalls and several toilets were located along that bulkhead, two or three decks above the hangar deck level. Many large pieces of metal had been blown through the head wall. The jagged edges of the holes had been cut out and the openings had been covered, from the elevator shaft side, by metal sheets welded over them. When taking a shower you couldn't help noticing the patches, four or five in each stall, and being

Kamikaze has just crashed through *Ticonderoga*'s flight deck in January 1945 attack. A casualty lies at left. Below, the island after the attack. The ship, repaired, refitted, and with a new crew, including the author, returned to action on April 21, 1945. (U.S. Navy photos.)

Wreckage in the officers head after the 1945 attack. (U.S. Navy photo.)

glad you weren't taking a shower, when metal flew through the wall.

From Bremerton we went south, along the coast to San Francisco. We couldn't have arrived at a more opportune time. We were there, at the Alameda Naval Air Station, from April 23rd until the 26th, during the organizational meeting of the United Nations. I saved a copy of the *San Francisco Chronicle*, an extra edition, of April 26, 1945. It said that

President Truman, by radio from Washington, addressed the opening session on the 25th and asked the delegates to remember the ideals for peace of the late President Roosevelt, who had died a few days before. Our Secretary of State Edward Stettinius, British Foreign Secretary Anthony Eden, Soviet Foreign Commissar V. M. Molotov, and China's Foreign Minister T. V. Soong were the "Big Four" representatives at the meetings. The Secretary General of the meeting was Alger Hiss. The first plenary session was to take place on the 26th when delegates from 46 nations would assemble at the Opera House.

I didn't go near the Opera House, only knowing, as usual, what I read in the newspapers; but one night I did visit the Fairmont Hotel, where the marble, columned lobby with its enormous oriental rugs was filled with sheikhs, African chiefs, Indians, and other delegates in colorful native dress. The newspaper reported that the Dow Jones industrials closed on April 25th at 163.91. Ads in the paper said that Beatrice Lillie was appearing in a play, and Yehudi Menuhin was to appear on the 28th. Tickets for the Menuhin concert were priced from $1.20 to a top of $4.80, tax included.

The ship was docked at the naval air station at Alameda, across the bay from San Francisco. On April 26th we backed, with the aid of tugboats, from our pier, slipped under the Bay Bridge, past Alcatraz, beneath the Golden Gate Bridge and headed southwesterly for Pearl. We arrived in Oahu on May 1st and went out for a six-day air and gunnery training session on the 3rd.

The *Honolulu Star-Bulletin* for May 2nd, which I saved, announced in three-inch headlines that "BERLIN FALLS TO RED ARMIES." An Associated Press dispatch from London said that Premier Stalin announced today the capture of Berlin. A United Press bulletin, also from London, quoted high military authorities as saying they did not believe that German military resistance would last long after the fall of Berlin. Other dispatches announced the unconditional surrender of " . . .approximately one million Axis troops in northern Italy and southern and western Austria." President Truman, at a news conference, announced that, ". . . according to the best possible information obtainable at this time, it is true that Hitler is dead." The Truman dispatch went on to say that: "The German radio announced to the world yesterday that Hitler—arch criminal of the Nazi regime and the man who led the Germans into the biggest (sic) war of all times—had died at his command post in the reichschancellery as the Russians surged through the capital in a final climactic battle." The story ended with: "Some doubt was expressed as to the authenticity of the German report, but Mr. Truman's assertion seemed to remove all questions from the minds of observers."

VE Day (Victory in Europe Day) was announced on May 8th. We left for Ulithi and our war on the 11th, but with the end of the war in Europe, maybe "they" would send us some of the European units to hasten the end of the Pacific war. By the end of May, my 24th birthday, we were back in combat with strikes on Okinawa, the Ryukyus, and southern Kyushu. There was a lot of war still to come, but with a difference. Air attacks on the fleet were almost exclusively kamikaze attacks.

The kamikazes were one-way suicide missions. For a time they were very successful and did tremendous damage to individual ships, as witness that to the *Ticonderoga* in January. The Japanese had run out of experienced pilots and were using the kamikazes as a desperation, terror weapon. They were terrifying, but were fought with increased fighter cover to down them before they arrived at an attack position, and intense antiaircraft fire if they did.

I'll never forget one attack. My battle station on the *Ticonderoga* was at "Sky 2," the gun control station at the aft end of the top of the island. From there, with phones and manual alarm switches, I had control of the 40mm guns on the starboard quarter of the ship. During one attack, with the ship firing everything we had, a kamikaze dove almost vertically directly at us. A fighter must have hit him on the way down; he was leaving a trail of smoke. Somebody's AA fire exploded him out of control and he splashed a couple of hundred yards away.

June was occupied with more strikes on southern Japan and Okinawa, where enemy resistance finally ended on June 22nd.[36] The end of June found *Ticonderoga* in Leyte Gulf where we had come for replenishment.

The author standing officer-of-the-deck watch on port wing of *Ticonderoga*'s bridge. Telescope-looking instrument is a pelorus, used to take visual bearings of ships or objects. A crosshair appears on the compass below the telescope.

During our stay I got ashore on the island of Leyte.

During the last few months the officers' summer uniform had been changed. The old uniform, which we had been wearing for the last two years, consisted of a long-sleeved cotton shirt, open at the neck; long cotton pants; and a pointed, overseas cap. All were tan or khaki-colored. An order had come from Washington that the new uniform was to be of the same material but the tan color was to replaced by a dark gray color.[37] Thousands of officers in the Pacific had a few sets of the tan uniforms. Since the new grays were not available in our areas, the "word" was that Admiral Nimitz had secured from Admiral King, in Washington, permission to use our old uniforms until they wore out. They never did. Since the Army had khaki shirts and pants in their PXs (post exchanges), when we needed new clothing we went to the nearest Army PX and bought it.

When we reached Leyte I needed some new pants and shirts. There was an Army PX on the island. The *Ticonderoga* and other ships of the task group were anchored about a mile offshore, beyond the range of malaria-bearing mosquitoes. A few friends and I got permission to go ashore to the PX, so we caught a ride in one of the LCVPs (landing craft, vehicle or personnel) that were being used as work boats in the anchorage. We carried canteens and K-rations for food and drink.

Ashore we found some kind of transportation and headed through Tacloban, a native village, for the army post. As I recall, the town had one street, lined with native huts of bamboo or scrap lumber, with straw or rusty tin roofs. Ditches containing sewage, waste water, and garbage bordered the muddy streets. No exotic south sea island, the place looked and smelled terrible. We bought our pants and shirts and returned to the ship. General MacArthur was welcome to Tacloban, and Leyte, too.

We left Leyte on the 1st of July heading for Japan, but shortly after leaving the ship had a problem with one of its engines and we went into Apra Harbor at Guam. We remained at Guam from the 5th to the 19th while a replacement part was flown out and installed. The island had some fine beaches and we got ashore several times. One of my trips was to the Air Force base which, at the time, was launching B-29 raids on Japan. The field on Guam, with strips on Saipan and Tinian Islands, would send hundreds of bombers over Japan each night. The planes did enormous damage to the enemy industrial capacity and to the cities where it was located. The atom-bomb planes, which eventually ended the war, flew from one of the bases in the Marianas.

The B-29 operations were marvels of logistic planning. The planes took off one by one down runways that appeared to be about two miles long. When one plane would get about halfway down the runway and its prop wash had dissipated, the next would have taxied into position and started its run. The planes, heavily loaded with bombs and gasoline, would use most of the runway before they would lift slowly off the strip. Since Japan was a couple of thousand miles away, and fuel economy was critical, the planes would not circle to join in formation. Each flew alone on its long round trip. The takeoffs lasted for hours.

A *Ticonderoga* plane crashes into the sea, close aboard. The pilot was lost. (U.S. Navy photo.)

As I remember, they began taking off at about noon. They were still taking off when I left at about 3, and I was told the last wouldn't get off until about 5. The next morning they would begin returning at about 6 a.m., the last ones landing about 11 a.m. Two parallel runways were in use the day I watched the takeoffs. To conserve fuel, only four or five planes at a time would be in the takeoff line. Later planes were readied, loaded, and started according to a tight time schedule.

The bombing runs were said to be mostly unopposed by this time in the war. Few fighters would meet them and antiaircraft fire was sporadic and below the bombers' altitudes. In fact several friends from the ship got overnight passes and went on runs. I didn't try to go, figuring my luck had held so far and there was no use tempting fate.

I did go aboard a parked B-29. They were our largest, four-engined bombers. The pressurized forward, control area was connected with the pressurized rear, gunnery and living compartment by a tube over the unpressurized bomb bay. The tube was a metal cylinder about 40 inches in diameter in which a man could lie on a wheeled sled and pull himself

One fighter taxis up deck after landing on *Ticonderoga*. Another takes wave-off until landing area is cleared. Five-inch gun barrels are in foreground. Below, a dive bomber has missed arresting wires and is about to crash into cable barriers. (U.S. Navy photos.)

along an overhead cable the 50 or 60 feet between the two compartments. On long flights crew members could sleep, eat, and use the toilet facilities in the rear compartment.

When *Ticonderoga* left the harbor at Guam the ship made a most unusual maneuver. The harbor was small with a narrow opening to the north and the sea. The ship had swung on its anchor to a westward heading. We had to head north to reach the exit channel and there wasn't enough space for the ship to hoist the anchor and get enough speed and steerageway to turn the ship northward. There must not have been enough tugs to position the ship normally. Four or five of our planes were tied down, wings folded, facing outboard along the aft port side of the flight deck. The anchor was left in place. The plane engines were started, revved up, and the pull of the plane propellers slowly pulled our stern 90 degrees. When the ship was headed north the anchor was weighed and we steamed northward under our own power and steerageway.

On July 21st we joined the fleet northeast of Iwo Jima. On the 24th and 25th we engaged in strikes on Kure and Kobe, and my date list says that we were 105 miles south of the Japanese island of Shikoku. On July 30th we made our first strike on Tokyo.

On August 6 a radio broadcast by President Truman stated that an atomic bomb had been dropped on Hiroshima. None of us had ever heard of such a bomb, but when it was said to have been the equivalent of 20,000 tons of TNT we realized it was something new and awesome. Another bomb was dropped a day or two later. On the 9th came the news that Russia had entered the war, probably we guessed, to pick up some of the pieces of Japan. On the 9th and 10th we made strikes on northern Honshu, Aomori, and Ominato.[38]

My notes read: "Aug 10 9:15 PM 'Radio SF has just announced that the Japanese Govt wish to surrender according to our ultimatum.'" On the 11th we were fueling at sea while a typhoon was brewing. It must have gone off to the northeast because that is my last mention of that typhoon. On the 13th we had strikes on Tokyo, and while at general quarters 15 Japanese planes were shot down. On August 14th we were fueling again and my notes say that there were unconfirmed reports of a

Japanese reply to a note from Secretary of State James Byrnes.

The war ended on August 15th! My notes say that a scheduled strike on Tokyo was called off at 0645. At 0800 we had news of U.S. acceptance of the reply to the terms of the Byrnes note. Seven enemy planes were splashed by the Third Fleet during the day and we were at battle stations from approximately 1000 to 1600.

After the war, before I left the *Ticonderoga*, I acquired copies of several messages received by the ship on August 15th.

These read as follows:

From: Commander Task Force 38

Action: ALL CARRIERS TF 38 Time of Receipt 0051.

SHOW TO ALL PILOTS X THE FACT THAT WE ARE ORDERED TO STRIKE INDICATES THAT THE ENEMY MAY HAVE THROWN AN UNACCEPTABLE JOKER INTO THE SURRENDER TERMS X THIS WAR COULD LAST MANY MONTHS LONGER X WE CANNOT AFFORD TO RELAX X NOW IS THE TIME TO POUR IT ON.

From: Commander Third Fleet (Halsey)

Action: All Stations This Circuit TOR 0635

WE HAVE RECEIVED INSTRUCTIONS FROM CINCPAC TO SUSPEND AIR ATTACK OPERATIONS.

From: Commander Third Fleet TOR 0754

Action: CTG 38.1/CTG 38.3/CTG 38.5/CTG 38.4 LI 6

THE NIP OFFICERS ARE STILL FIGHTING X THAT MEANS WE ARE STILL FACING THE ENEMY THAT HATES OUR CARRIERS LIKE THE DEVIL HATES HOLY WATER X UNTIL THEY SURRENDER AND ARE DISARMED REPEAT DISARMED THEY ARE DANGEROUS AND NEED KILLING X THE BEST PRESENT INSURANCE FOR OUR FORCES AND FUTURE INSURANCE FOR PEACE IS TO CARRY IT TO THEM WITH EVERY THING WE HAVE X CARRY ON X HALSEY.

From: CINCPAC CINCPOA [Commander-in-Chief Pacific Fleet. Commander-in-Chief Pacific Ocean Areas. Nimitz]
Action: PACFLT - RDO FRISCO - RDO *Washington* - SECNAV.TOR 1506 CINCPOA COMMUNIQUE #467

ORDERS HAVE BEEN ISSUED TO THE U S PACIFIC FLEET AND TO OTHER FORCES UNDER THE COMMAND OF THE COMMANDER IN CHIEF U S PACIFIC FLEET AND PACIFIC OCEAN AREAS TO CEASE OFFENSIVE OPERATIONS AGAINST THE JAPANESE.

OFFICIALLY, the war was over. The air strikes and antiaircraft firing stopped, but there were other operations for Task Force 38 and the *Ticonderoga*. Immediately following the end of the war, possibly as early as August 16th, the ship received an order to form a "Landing Force" to

The author's platoon was part of an amphibious assault battalion, shown here on the *Ticonderoga* flight deck August 21, 1945. It did not get ashore for occupation duty. (U.S. Navy photo.)

be landed in Japan and form a guard or occupying force. Other carriers, presumably, formed similar units. When ashore all units from all the ships would be sent to designated areas for initial occupation duties. Two of the places to be occupied were Atsugi Air Base, southwest of Tokyo, and the large navy base on Tokyo Bay at Yokosuka.

The universal advice at any military or naval base was: 'Never volunteer for anything.' This was one time I broke that rule. To have been among the first Americans to land in Japan would have been a real adventure. I volunteered and was one of seven officers and 170 men in our group. We organized, were equipped, and drilled on the flight deck, but when the time came our mission was cancelled, although our Marine detachment was sent ashore. Our naval contingent was disappointed, but we had a great time for a couple of weeks.

I saved a handful of mimeographed sheets relating to our landing force. The unit had a commanding officer, an executive officer, a doctor, and four junior officers in charge of four platoons. I was commander of the first platoon which contained about 40 men.

One batch of 16 legal-sized, single-spaced sheets described our duties and how to perform them. Headings like: commander of the guard; field officer of the day; corporal of the guard; tours; watches; duties of personnel; sentinels; general orders; prisoners and prisoner guards covered every eventuality we might encounter and how to handle it. Other sheets listed equipment which included rifles for the men, .45 caliber pistols for the officers, helmets, gas masks, and a sea bag to carry extra clothing and personal gear. A final memory was of the entire company in formation on the flight deck (see photo, page 139). We were ready to go when the mission was scrubbed.

CHAPTER 15

Tokyo Bay

AFTER our offensive operations stopped on August 15th, the next two or three weeks saw the Nimitz CinCPac-CinCPoa and MacArthur Southwest Pacific Area staffs planning occupation forces for Japan, organizing the transportation of diplomats and military people to the surrender ceremony, and planning the surrender itself aboard the *USS Missouri*, our newest *Iowa*-class battleship and flagship of Admiral Halsey.

On the *Ticonderoga* we were informed of news events by a mimeographed news sheet called, at different times, the *Daily News* or *Daily Press*. A special news bulletin from our captain, William Sinton, dated and inscribed marginally by me on August 22, 1945, outlined the plans for the surrender of and initial occupation of Japan. In it he mentioned that the *Cowpens* would be the first carrier to enter Tokyo Bay to set up an emergency naval air station ashore. Our Naval Landing Force, which didn't land, was to occupy Yokosuka Naval Base on the 28th. The remainder of the fast carriers, numbering possibly a dozen, would remain offshore flying combat air patrols from the Tokyo area all the way back to Okinawa. Nobody trusted the Japanese. Our guns were kept loaded and ready. The airborne CAP fighters were ready for instant combat.

When the surrender was signed on September 2nd, the skies within a 50-mile radius around the *Missouri* were loaded with armed fighter planes and the ships' air search radars were scanning the area.

My record shows that we anchored in Tokyo Bay on September 6th and remained there until the 20th. We were anchored off the Yokosuka Naval Base which was on the west side of the bay about 30 miles south of Tokyo. I went ashore a few times in the Yokosuka area, and once got up to Tokyo.

Japanese sign surrender documents aboard *USS Missouri*, BB-63, in Tokyo Bay, September 2, 1945. General MacArthur is at left, behind microphone. Admiral Halsey, wearing soft cap, is in center of first row of officers beyond table. (U.S. Navy photo.)

The trip to Tokyo was the memorable one. I made the trip with two other junior officers. The armed forces exchange rate for Japanese currency was 15 yen for one dollar; we were allowed to take 150 yen ashore. With our yen, individual canteens of water, and a K-ration each, since we would be gone all day, we set out.

A LCVP landed us at a dock at the Yokosuka base, or what was left of it. It had been one of the main bases for the Japanese fleet. It was pretty well wrecked. What had been large brick buildings were now large piles of rubble. There wasn't an undamaged building in the area. A few main streets had been cleared, but only the shells of buildings and jumbles of timbers and brick remained. A bus, brought in by our forces and driven by a sailor, took us through the wreckage to the railroad station in the town.

The railway was a spur off the main line which ran through the heavily populated areas of Tokyo through Yokohama to the southwest. The Yokosuka station and tracks were intact and in use by large numbers of people. We were told that the railway had, purposefully, not been bombed so it could be used after the war. As I recall, it was a double-tracked electric line powered by overhead cables. It reminded me of the tracks that ran between Washington and New York in the 1940s. The roadbed was clean, well maintained, and in excellent condition.

In the station crowds of Japanese civilians waited to board the trains. Uniformed train guards had the civilians stand back, and motioned us through to our northbound train. We boarded our car with two or three other groups of U.S. officers, reversed one of the movable, cane-upholstered seats and sat down. When all the Americans were aboard, the Japanese were allowed to enter the car, which quickly filled to standing room only. I could feel the Japanese staring at us, but when we looked at them their eyes were elsewhere. The center aisle was packed with standing Japanese. When the train was filled there was a whistle and the cars slid quietly out of the station.

The train increased its speed; the power poles zipped by faster and faster until the speed leveled off at I'd guess, about 50 m.p.h. The train went through an industrial area, with small buildings everywhere and very little open land. I would feel Japanese eyes on us, look in that direction, and see expressionless faces looking somewhere else. I thought for a moment that these people, if they wished, could have stuck knives into us, thrown us off the train, and we couldn't have done a thing about it. But they had been told the war was over; they were not to interfere with us; and no one dared question the instruction. I guessed that they were as curious about us as we were about them. I felt completely safe packed in among the hundreds of Japanese.

We were seated on the right side of the train with a clear view from our large window. We could see nothing to the left because of the aisle packed with standees. After about 10 minutes of seeing damaged buildings go by, probably in Yokohama, we entered an unusual area which, a map showed later, was in the southern part of Tokyo. A sea of bent, twisted tin sheets covered the ground for as far as I could see. Interspersed among the miles of tin were upright, rectangular shapes, maybe two or three feet high, sitting on earth or concrete bases. Closer looks at the shapes revealed that they were iron safes. Nothing else was in sight—just the layer of twisted gray, maybe a foot or two thick, stretching to the horizon. There were no tree trunks, no power poles poking out of the flat plain; only the silent sea of tin, sprinkled with the black safes under a vast expanse of sky.

The area evidently had been burned after an incendiary bombing raid. The expanse must have been covered with lightly built housing roofed with tin sheets. Each family must have kept its most valued possessions in the individual safes. What a fire it must have been. The bleak scene passed at the speed of the train for minute after minute until, it seemed, it would never stop.

It wasn't until recently that I understood what we had seen. It was what remained after one of the most terrible tragedies of the war. On March 9th, hundreds of B-29s dropped thousands of incendiary bombs in the flat, southern part of Tokyo. The resulting fire storm took the lives of between 100,000 and 200,000 people. There were many more deaths than occurred in Hamburg, Germany, in 1943, when 30,000 died in a fire storm after a bombing attack.[39]

Fire storms are caused, I have read, by the winds created by enormous fires. On a scale that is easier to understand, they are like the fire that occurs after a large bonfire is ignited. After the fire is well underway, with plenty of dry, unburned fuel to be consumed, the bonfire creates its own uncontrolled, roaring draft. A city-sized fire creates a whirling tornado of wind consuming everything in its path until it runs out of fuel. The Tokyo fire storm was said to have covered 17 square miles. All that remained was the sea of twisted tin, pimpled with the blackened safes, a silent testament to the fire storm of all-out war.

I don't remember the railroad station in Tokyo, but I do recall catching a ride in a weapons carrier, a pickup truck-like vehicle with a canvas cover over the cargo box. One of us rode in the front passenger seat with the driver, the others in the rear. The army enlisted driver said he was supposed to be inspecting for mosquitoes, but he wasn't averse to inspecting while taking us sight-seeing. As I recall, downtown Tokyo had many bombed-out areas, but here and there would be untouched buildings of eight or 10 stories. There was no traffic on the streets but our military vehicles: a few trucks and jeeps. The long street beside the Emperor's palace compound paralleled a water-filled moat. Across the moat was a massive brick wall, and willow trees, at intervals, overhung the wall. We were told that the compound had been off-limits for our bombers; that for political and psychological reasons, the Emperor and his compound had been carefully avoided.

Our truck parked, finally, across the street from the Imperial Hotel. The landmark building, designed by Frank Lloyd Wright, was being used as some kind of Army headquarters. It was, I recall, a low, red-brick building, rectangular and modern in the architectural style of the twenties, when it was built. Inside, the lobby, public rooms and corridors were dimly lit with battery lamps or Coleman lanterns. Electric power had not been restored to that area of the city. After a brief look at that dim interior, we retired to our vehicle across the street. To the right of our truck was an area with trees and open space. We were parked by a park.

Before continuing on our way we sat in the rear of the truck and ate our K-rations which, as I recall, consisted of small cans of deviled ham or Spam, cheese, packages of soda crackers, a candy bar, a few sticks of gum, and a few cigarettes. In the middle of our picnic we noticed unusual activity. By ones and twos, Japanese men, some accompanied by a child, arrived on the sidewalk to watch us eat. There were, probably, five or six adults and half a dozen children. They just stood there, without expression, and watched us silently. It dawned on us that they were waiting for us to throw away what we didn't eat. They were hungry and were waiting for our scraps. That ended our meal. We gave what was left: crackers, candy, and chewing gum to the children, the cigarettes to the men. There was no scramble for the food. Each took what was given quietly, without expression, but, I think, thankfully. When all was dispensed, they departed down the sidewalk as they had come, by ones and twos, perhaps to find other GIs with something to eat.

Another experience in Tokyo sticks in my memory. We wanted to

The author, right, with an unidentified sailor, in front of the former Bank of Okinawa, Naha, Okinawa, 1945. When this picture was taken, most of the island had been secured, but Japanese resistance continued on the southern portion.

buy some souvenirs, but there was not much to be had. On the sidewalks outside closed former department stores, street vendors displayed such wares as shoe laces; paper items like napkins or scratch pads; and plastic combs. Nothing to take home as a remembrance of Tokyo. Finally we came to a small shop lined with shelves bearing ceramic tablets with Japanese letters on them. The tablets were about six or eight inches high, on small china bases, and were glazed in black or white enamel. The letters, in black or gold, had been baked onto some of the tablets. Other tablets, apparently, awaited their lettering.

We asked the shopkeeper for his prices. He spoke no English and from his excited manner and shaking head we gathered the tablets were not for sale. We insisted. He became more excited. At last he disappeared into the back of the shop and returned with a catalog. He showed us a picture of a shrine in a Japanese home. The shelves of the shrine displayed a few of the tablets. They were memorials for deceased family members to be kept in individual homes. The letters were the names of the dead. We left him with his tablets, embarrassed by our ignorance.

Among my meager supply of Japanese souvenirs, I found the front page of *The Mainichi*, an English-language newspaper published in Osaka on September 15, 1945.[40] To the left of a photo of the Potsdam Conference, showing Truman, Churchill, and Stalin, is a statement by General MacArthur. After saying that, "Japan has sunk to the status of a fourth-rate military power . . . ," he added that, "It will . . . be . . . impossible for Japan . . . to become a leading country of the world." The rear of the same sheet[41] had ads by large manufacturing, insurance, and communications companies. They admonished their countrymen to: "Build New Japan With Renewed Vigor!" and "Do Your Best For Construction Of A Bright Japan!"

The *Ticonderoga* sailed from Tokyo Bay on September 20th. Our course was a great circle one to Oahu; we zigzagged no more. At night our lights must have looked like a cruise ship's. We docked on Ford Island, Pearl, on the 28th. As the ship was secured to the dock, a Navy band played and a chorus of WAVES sang a welcome. At last, the war was over. We were headed home.

CHAPTER 16

The "Magic Carpet"

ON the long trip, from Tokyo to Pearl, the fact finally sank in that the war, after all the years, was really over. The Navy wouldn't need me any longer, and I certainly was ready to be discharged, to go home and begin a more normal life. A few million other servicemen had the same idea. The demobilization of so many people, with so much equipment, in so many places apparently took the various services some time to organize.

The Navy had a personnel demobilization plan based on a point system. When you accumulated enough points you could be discharged. Points were given for marital status, dependents, age, and length of service. By any method of tabulating I had insufficient points to get out. I was unmarried, had no dependents, was 24 years old, and my length of service was not unusual. I wasn't going home for about eight months, as it happened, but I wasn't being kamikaze-ed at either, and we were heading for the States on a new duty, ferrying troops from the Pacific to the west coast.

The troopship duty was named operation "Magic Carpet." Our first run was immediate. We had arrived in Pearl on September 28th. On the 30th we left for San Francisco with a load of servicemen. After a few days at the Alameda Naval Air Station, we returned to Pearl and then made a run to Puget Sound, Seattle, and Tacoma, Washington. On October 27th we had open house, for Navy Day, in Tacoma. The *Tacoma Times* for October 23, 1945, said: "Battle weary and worn, but still pugnacious and defiant, the navy's beloved 'Big T'—the USS *Ticonderoga* (CV-14) . . . dropped her hook in Tacoma waters Monday afternoon . . . bearing 967 enlisted men and 97 officers, overseas army men who had gone aboard at Oahu, T. H. . . . for transfer to the states for discharge." Other ships expected, the paper said, were the battleship *USS Maryland*, the cruiser *USS Atlanta*, and the submarines *USS Entemedor* and *USS Stickleback*. A destroyer, *USS Norman Scott*, was already in port. A picture in the paper showed our flight deck covered with planes, which the caption said were "gradually being transferred to other duty, as the navy has ordered the 'T' readied for transport duty . . ." Tacoma must have had a great Navy Day. Several thousand visited aboard the "T," but most of the men on the *Ticonderoga* couldn't wait to hit the beach in the sailor's never-ending quest for wine, women and song.

From Tacoma we returned to Pearl and the "Magic Carpet" duty began in earnest. All our planes, the airgroups, and "airedales" left the ship. Welders came aboard and covered our hangar deck with steel pipe bunks, four bunks high. The forest of bunks on the acres of hangar deck could sleep several thousand men. With the thousand or more ship's spaces vacated by the airmen, we could transport four or five thousand GIs per trip. As soon as the last bunk was in place, we headed for Samar Island, in the Philippines, for our first load of returnees.

The wardroom mess, where the ship's officers ate their meals, was organized in the normal Navy way. Officers paid a mess bill each month into a common fund; the fund bought food for the mess from Navy supplies; the food was cooked by Navy personnel in the wardroom galley and eaten in the wardroom dining room, both Navy properties. The quasi-independent mess must have been organized to permit activities other than the official feeding of the officers, probably social events ashore.

Our mess used its independence wisely. It, or we, acquired three slot machines — old-time "one-armed-bandits" — and sacks of change to feed them. One machine took nickels, one dimes, and one quarters. Of our thousands of passengers, possibly a thousand were officers who ate in the wardroom. Those men had been overseas for months or years and were loaded with cash. They had nothing to do all day or night except eat, sleep, and play our slots. The machines ran day and night. When one broke down it was taken to the machine shop and fixed immediately.

The *Ticonderoga* enters San Francisco Bay after the war. Flight deck, hangar deck openings, gun tubs, and catwalks are covered with GIs returning to the states.

The saying, "Time is money" never proved more true. We paid no mess bills during our "Magic Carpet" days. There was serious talk of a wardroom mess dividend.

We brought our Philippine passengers to San Francisco. The "T" steamed majestically into the Golden Gate channel at about mid-morning on a crisp day. Everyone not on duty was topside to see what they had anticipated for months. The flight deck was loaded with GIs. The gun tubs, catwalks, and the island were covered with men. A few hundred yards from the Golden Gate Bridge a faint cry was heard. In a few seconds we located its source: a lone sailor was leaning over the railing high overhead in the center of the bridge, waving his hat wildly and shouting a welcome. The thousands of men on the ship spotted the sailor at the same time and with a tremendous roar returned his greeting. It was a welcome to remember.

We made another trip across the Pacific for a load of GIs. That time it was to Okinawa. The last two notes in my non-journal are: "6 Jan [1946] Lv Buckner Bay, Okinawa . . . 20 Jan Ar. San Francisco." I was released from active duty in New Orleans on April 4, 1946.

I have no record of what happened between January and April 1946. We may have made another trip to Pearl, but I think not. I do remember the ship going into the Bremerton Navy Yard where we put the ship in "moth balls," permanent storage. The ship's crew was moved ashore into navy yard housing. Open gun mounts were covered with dome-shaped, wooden frames. A network of plastic tape was placed over the frames and liquid fiber glass was sprayed over the tape. The result was a weather-proof, airtight dome. A silica gel dessicant was placed inside the dome before sealing it and the guns would be kept dry, and, ostensibly, operable for several years. Enclosed turrets and inside spaces were preserved by greasing operating parts and simply closing and sealing the compartment. When I left the ship I never expected to see the *Ticonderoga* again, but I did later, on television, when it was used as a recovery ship for some of the early space program landings. She was scrapped in 1973.

According to my reference book on U.S. aircraft carriers,[42] all of the nine CVLs of the *Independence*-class, including the *Cowpens*, have been sunk or scrapped with one having been sold to Spain in 1967, and two leased to France. Of the 26 wartime carriers of the *Essex*-class, including *Ticonderoga*, all but six have been scrapped. One of these, the second *Yorktown*, is a museum ship at Charleston, South Carolina; another, the *Intrepid*, at New York. The second *Lexington* was used as a training ship for years; was decommissioned in November 1991, and, in January 1992, was towed to Corpus Christi, Texas, to be preserved as a museum ship. Four ships, according to my reference, were said to be in reserve status, but the wire services, at the time of the *Lexington*'s decommissioning, in 1991, referred to it as the last of the World War II carriers.

On April 4, 1946, I was released from active duty in New Orleans, detached, and ordered to proceed home. I was granted a month and 20 days leave, after which on May 24, 1946, I was released from active duty. My notice of separation states that I had been awarded the following campaign medals: American Defense Service; American Theater of War;

Asiatic-Pacific Area (10 stars); World War Two Victory Medal; Philippine Liberation (2 stars). [43]

My "jacket," like those of millions of other servicemen, includes a "Certificate of Satisfactory Service." Mine is dated October 24, 1946. Other separation documents include a form letter from then-Secretary of the Navy James Forrestal, and a printed thank-you from ". . . a grateful Nation" from President Truman. I appreciated the thoughts, then and now.[44]

In a Bureau of Naval Personnel letter, dated October 24, 1946, I was notified that the *Cowpens* had been awarded a Navy Unit Commendation "for outstanding heroism displayed by her crew in action against enemy Japanese forces . . ." during certain periods of the war, and that I was authorized to wear, as part of my uniform, the Navy Unit Commendation ribbon.[45]

On February 10, 1949, I was promoted, permanently, to full Lieutenant, USNR, having been promoted as a temporary Lieutenant on April 1, 1946, before leaving the *Ticonderoga* on April 2nd. On July 1, 1961, I was transferred to the Retired Reserve.

I placed that final notice in my "jacket" of official Navy papers and thought my naval connections were, at last, over. They were not. A postscript was to come.

CHAPTER 17

Another *Cowpens*

IN the 1980s I saw a newspaper story of a *USS Cowpens* reunion to be held at Cowpens, South Carolina. I wrote for an application, joined the organization, and have been on its mailing list ever since. I have attended one meeting, held in nearby Spartanburg, a larger town, to accommodate the approximately 300 reunioners and wives. My old shipmate, Ken Maudsley, was there and we have kept in touch ever since.

On the site of the battle, five miles from Spartanburg, the National Park Service has constructed a visitors' center to mark the Cowpens National Battlefield and to house a slide and sound exhibit which graphically describes the 1781 battle.

In January 1991, I received an invitation from Bath, Maine, where the ship was built, to the commissioning of another *USS Cowpens,* CG-63, a guided missile cruiser. The event would take place at the Charleston, South Carolina, Navy Yard on March 9th. My wife and I were on the pier, with about 5,000 others, at the proper time.

It was a typical spring day in the South: partly sunny and cool, about 60 degrees, flags and pennants snapping gently in a light breeze. The ship was moored to a wide, concrete pier with bleachers and hundreds of folding chairs for the spectators. The sparkling new cruiser was dressed with pennants and signal flags from stem to stern; the rails and gangways were covered with red, white, and blue bunting. While the crowd gathered and found seats, a band played Souza marches.

A speakers' stand had been placed on the main deck, amidships, facing the bleachers and seats on the pier. A special section, for former CVL-25 returnees, was near front and center. The speaking began and, after a while, I thought it might never end. The Persian Gulf War had ended a few days before and each speaker was compelled to refer to our technology, dedication, and patriotism in its speedy conclusion. All of which was fine to hear the first time, but when the third and subsequent speakers hit the same chords it got pretty dreary. The main speaker was the admiral vice chairman of the joint chiefs of staff. Others included the state's two U.S. senators, three representatives, the mayors of Charleston and Cowpens, a few people from the Bath Iron Works Corporation, which built the ship, and a member of the original *Cowpens* crew.

After about two hours of earnest, endless verbiage, the moment arrived. The colors were paraded, the ensign was raised on the stern staff, the commissioning pennant was broken from the foremast, and the ship became a part of the U.S. Navy. The commanding officer read the order to set the first watch, the executive officer set the watch, and the ship "came alive" as the crew, led by officers with unsheathed swords, ran up the gangways and manned the rails from the maindeck to the levels highest on the superstructure. Smoke came from the ship's stacks, a 19-gun salute was fired from the end of the next slip, and the ship was opened to visitors.

What a ship she is! The following data comes from the program printed for the occasion. CG-63 is an Aegis guided-missile cruiser, so called because of the "Aegis" computer-controlled, phased-array radar system. Unlike our old radar systems which sent out a single beam from a 360-degree antenna rotation, the new system sounds out its beams in all directions simultaneously. Hundreds of targets may be tracked and targeted continuously, or the system may be used to direct fighter aircraft or helicopters to protect the ship or group.

The ship's firepower is awesome. Beneath the forward and after parts of the maindeck are vertical missile launch tubes, 122 in all, each covered by a hatch cover. The missiles carried may be any combination of Tomahawk, Harpoon, or other missiles, the proper missile and tube for an air, surface, or land target selected and directed by the computer operators. The scuttlebutt during the Gulf War said a Tomahawk could hit a tennis court two hundred miles away. Harpoons, the program said, fly at very low altitudes, beneath the beams of air-search radars, so are important anti-ship weapons.

The new *Cowpens*, 1991, at her commissioning. The hatch covers in foreground cover the aft battery of vertical missile tubes. The covers open automatically and an assortment of air, surface, and land attack missiles may be fired from the ship's combat information center. At the rear of the photo, beneath the netting, is a wheeled missile launcher, circa the Battle of Cowpens era.

For antisubmarine operations, the ship has two sonar systems, one in the bow and another which may be towed. Underwater targets may be found and tracked by the systems and destroyed by ship-launched torpedoes.

Two helicopters are carried by the ship, extending the radar and surveillance systems by hundreds of miles. For short range firepower, the ship has two five-inch cannons and two 20mm weapons systems. Each 20mm Gatling gun has six barrels and can fire 4,500 rounds per minute.

Her array of weapons may be controlled, simultaneously, from a

The new *USS Cowpens*, CG-63, a *Ticonderoga*-class guided missile cruiser, at her commissioning, March 9, 1991, in Charleston, South Carolina. View is from her starboard quarter. Note the crew manning the rails, the helicopter pulled from its bay, and the array of electronic gear on her masts and superstructure.

CIC, combat information center, beneath the bridge. The bulkheads of the CIC compartment were lined with video screens of various sizes with computer keyboards in front of most of them. Nothing in the room resembled any equipment in the CICs of World War II. One screen was operating in the dimly lighted room. The picture on it panned from the bow of the ship, with its visitors, to the pier where chairs were being folded and stacked, to a tug passing in the harbor. Someone in the room was aiming the remote TV camera. I didn't notice where he was located.

The ship is 567 feet long; has a beam of 55 feet; a draft of 34 feet; a displacement of 9,600 tons; two reversible-pitch propellers; four gas turbine engines turning out 80,000 shaft horsepower. Speed is listed as "30+ knots." From the looks of her the plus-sign represents many more knots than the old *Cowpens,* which also was rated at 30+ knots. She is operated by 66 officers and 339 enlisted men. Before the disintegration of the Soviet Union, the new *Cowpens* was the 17th of 27 Aegis cruisers the Navy planned to buy.

The day's icing on the cake was my discovery that the *Cowpens* was the latest in the *Ticonderoga*-class of guided-missile cruisers. I haven't followed Navy news through the years, but I had heard that there was a new *Ticonderoga* and that it was a guided-missile cruiser. I had no idea that it was the first of the Aegis-equipped class until I read it in the commanding officer's welcome in the program. The new *Ticonderoga* is CG-47. As noted, I'm not much of a gambler, but I'd give most any odds that I was the only man within a thousand miles of Charleston, on March 9, 1991, who had wartime service on both World War II carriers.

Later in 1991 this naval tale finished in Pensacola, Florida, with the decommissioning of the last of the World War II carriers. The "new" *Lexington*, CV-16, of the *Essex*-class, was commissioned in 1943 and was named after the "old" *Lexington*, CV-2, which was sunk in the Battle of the Coral Sea in 1942.[46] In 1955 the "new" LEX was converted to a training carrier and was renumbered AVT-16, the AVT meaning aviation training. The landing area of her flight deck was canted to port and the supports under it were strengthened to take the weights and landing speeds of the larger jet aircraft being used in the fleet. She reported to the Pensacola Naval Air Station in 1962 and thousands of carrier pilots qualified aboard her during the following 29 years.

In March 1991, an Associated Press news story said that the final two training cruises of "the historic aircraft carrier Lexington" had been cancelled "because of maintenance problems, mounting repair costs and the Gulf War cease-fire." Captain Bill Kennedy, the *Lexington*'s skipper, said that problems with the ship's power plant and non-availability of parts were the main reasons for the cancellation.

The news story continued: "The honor of making the final landing went to Lt. Kathy Owens, 27, a native of Cincinnati, on March 8 while the ship was steaming about 45 miles south of Pensacola, its home port for the last 29 years." It was landing number 493,760 on the *Lexington*,

The author, center in hat, on flight deck of *Lexington*, Pensacola, April 1991. First glassed-in level, at left of photo, is admiral's flag bridge. Next level up is ship's operating bridge. Cylinder above bridges is base of former fire control director for forward five-inch turrets.

"more than any other carrier . . . Kennedy said it was noteworthy that a woman made the final landing aboard the ship affectionately known as the 'Lady Lex.'" Kennedy was a good sport. The news story said that he had planned to make the last landing himself, but when the *Lexington*'s machinery gave out and the ship couldn't go to sea for its last missions, the last landing happened to have been made by Lt. Owens. She had flown a heavy, twin-engined turboprop that was delivering mail, parts and cargo.

For many years my family and I have vacationed on the Gulf Coast just west of Pensacola. We were vacationing there in April 1991. On April 6 I went aboard the *Lexington* with my daughter. The ship was in her usual berth at a commercial pier in downtown Pensacola. She was much different from the old *Ticonderoga*. As there were no planes aboard, her hangar deck seemed more cavernous than I had remembered it. All of her guns had been removed long ago. The two five-inch turrets forward and two aft of her island were gone, making the profile of her island rise abruptly from the flight deck. The five-inch gun directors, forward and aft at the top of the island were gone, but their circular tracks were still visible. Her flight deck seemed larger than I recalled, perhaps because of the angled, after end of the deck. The landing areas had fittings for only four or five arresting wires, evidence of the greater precision of modern instrument landings. Where the landing signal officer had been located, there was now electronic, instrument-landing gear. What appeared to be a large box, maybe eight feet wide by five feet high and studded with six-inch cylinders, had replaced the LSO. The cylinders probably transmitted radio beams which helped direct the jets to their contacts with the arresting wires.

On May 3 my wife and I were again at our place on the Gulf. The *Pensacola News Journal* that day had a front page picture of the *Lexington* being moved by tugs from its downtown location. Her destination was a pier at the Naval Air Station, five miles down the bay. The paper said that for the last two years the ship had been berthed downtown so that the NAS basin and dock could be modified to accommodate the *USS Forrestal*, the replacement training carrier scheduled to arrive in 1992.

The *Lexington* being towed from Pensacola Harbor to her final resting place, May 1991.

The *Lexington* was decommissioned on November 8, 1991. The *Pensacola News Journal* of November 9th described the scene. A crowd estimated at 3,600 former crew members, skippers and fliers attended the "bittersweet" ceremony under cloudy skies with a 15 m.p.h. wind out of the north. The temperature was 45 degrees. There were flyovers by World War II Wildcats, SNJs, a TBM, and, finally, by jets of the Navy's Blue Angel precision flying team which is based at Pensacola.

A former mayor of Pensacola said, ". . . it's sad to see a part of our history come to a close at a time when so many Americans are renewing their patriotism." The Chief of Naval operations, Admiral Frank B. Kelso, said, ". . . We are marking the end of an era. . . ." The commission pennant was lowered. Crew members left the ship for the last time. "Taps played at the end."

The last of the eight pre-World War II carriers, the *Enterprise*, was withdrawn from service in 1947 and scrapped in 1959. The last of the *Independence*-class of CVLs was scrapped in 1970. Now the last of the *Essex*-class, the *Lexington*, was decommissioned. The last of the fast carriers of World War II had reached the end of the line. Admiral Kelso was right: it was, indeed, the end of an era—50 years of war and peace, of props and jets, of men and women, all connected by a succession of historic times and historic ships.[47]

APPENDIX 1

25 June Left Phila.
15 July Arr. Norfolk

18 July Left Norfolk
23 July Ar. Trinidad

7 Aug. Left Trinidad
11 Aug Ar. Phila

14 Aug – 19 Aug Leave Period

28 Aug Left Phila
2 Sept Ar Pan. Canal

2 Sept – 3 Sept Transit Pan. Can.

4 Sept Left Pan. Can.
11 Sept Ar. San Diego

13 Sept Left San Diego
19 Sept Ar. Pearl Harbor

29 Sept Left P.H.
Wake Island raid
14 Oct Ar. P.H

Abbot episode

9 Nov Left P.H.
Gilberts Invasion (Mili, Makin, Tarawa)
Marshalls attack (Dec 4) Kwajalein. Night attacks
8 Dec Ar. P.H.

1944

16 Jan Left P.H.
22 Jan Neptune Day)
31 Jan Eniwetok raided (Marshall invasion)
30 Jan Kwajalein raided
4 Feb Majuro Lagoon

12 Feb Left Majuro
16-17 Feb Truk raided
19 Feb night attack near Ponape
21st Feb Night attack going to Saipan
22 Feb Saipan, Tinian, Guam raided
25 Feb Ar. Majuro

28 Feb Left Majuro
4 Mar. Ar. Pearl

15 Mar Lv Pearl 20 Mar Ar Majuro
23 Mar Lv Majuro
29 Mar night attack — nite attack
30 Mar — Palau; 31 Mar Yap night attack
1 Apr. Woleai
6 Apr Ar Majuro

13 Apr Lv Majuro
21-22-23-24 Apr Hollandia invasion of Wakde Sawar airfields.
29 Apr. Truk attack
2 May Bombardment Ponape
4 May Ar. Kwajalein

crossed equator 12 times total

12 May (?) Lv Kwajalein
13 May ? Ar. Majuro

6 June Lv Majuro
12-13 June hit Saipan Tinian Guam Pagan
15 D day Marianas Invasion
16-17 June hit Iwo & Chichi Jima
19 June air battle near Rota
21-22 June Jap fleet hit & retired
4 July left for Eniwetok
6 July Ar Eniwetok

1st Phil. Sea

8 July Lv Eniwetok
10 July Ar Majuro
11 July Lv Majuro
15 July Ar Pearl Harbor

16 July – 10 Aug Yard period FDR arrives. SAS OOD on training runs.

10 Aug Lv Pearl Harbor
SAS OOD
29 Aug Lv Eniwetok
CROSSED EQUATOR
6-24 Aug hit Palau, Mindanao, Central P.I., Luzon, Menado Celebes, Morotai
Luzon. Air attack 24 Aug
28 Sept Ar. Manus (Seeadler)

2 Oct Lv. Manus
10 Oct OKINAWA, NANSEI SHOTOS
12 OCT FORMOSA
NITE ATTACK ON T.F. 38
13 OCT FORMOSA
DUSK ATTACK. 7 SHOT DOWN. CANBERRA HIT. WASP, HORN, COW, MONT. 5" AA OVER DECK
14 OCT VF SWEEP ON FORMOSA
DUSK ATTACK. HOUSTON HIT.
40 MM OVER DECK. " START ABANDON
15 OCT LEFT 38.1. JOIN CABOT AND CRUISERS. 60 odd Japs downed
16 OCT Cabot gets 32. Cow 9 planes.

U.S.S. COWPENS

Page from author's personal list of dates, places, and operations. Begins June 25, 1943, leaving Philadelphia aboard *Cowpens*.

APPENDIX 2

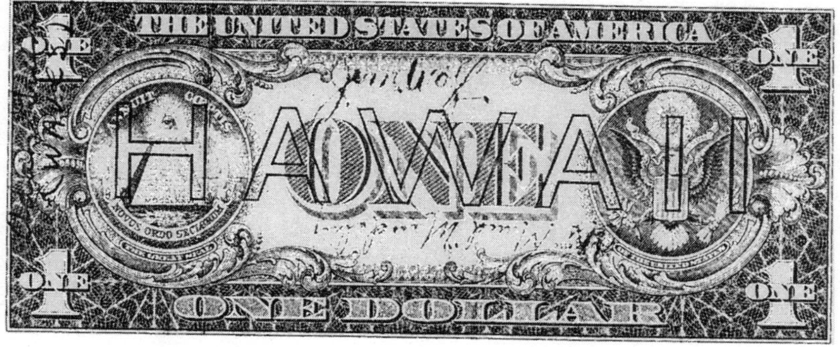

Author's "Hawaii" dollar bill, a souvenir of trip on the *Enterprise*, 1944. Front has dates and various signatures. Back has signatures of author's former college roommate, Jim Wolf, who was assigned to *Enterprise*, and "Maud" Maudsley, shipmate from *Cowpens*.

APPENDIX 3-A

U. S. S. TICONDEROGA

Heading:

SHOW TO ALL PILOTS X THE FACT THAT WE ARE ORDERED TO STRIKE INDICATES THAT THE ENEMY MAY HAVE THROWN AN UNACCEPTABLE JOKER INTO THE SURRENDER TERMS X THIS WAR COULD LAST MANY MONTHS LONGER X WE CANNOT AFFORD TO RELAX X NOW IS THE TIME TO POUR IT ON

TOR 00051 INFORMATION DATE 15 AUGUST

From: CTF38 | Precedence | Classification PLAIN | Radio TBS Visual | D-T-G NONE

Action: ALL CARRIERS TF38

Info: ALL TGC'S

Capt. •	Exec. •	Comm. •	Air X	Nav.	Gun.	Eng.	1st. Lieut.	Medical	Supply	Disb.	A. C. I. A	Radio	Air Plot X	C. I. C. X	Aero.	Capt. Off.	Exec. Off.	CTAG X	Duty Cdr.	O. O. D.	R. P. Cust.	Signal	Radar Mat.		C W. O.

• --Receives copy all messages. A --Action Officer X --Information Officer

Above and following three pages are copies, kept by author, of messages received from commanders of Pacific naval forces as the war was ending on August 15, 1945.

APPENDIX 3-B

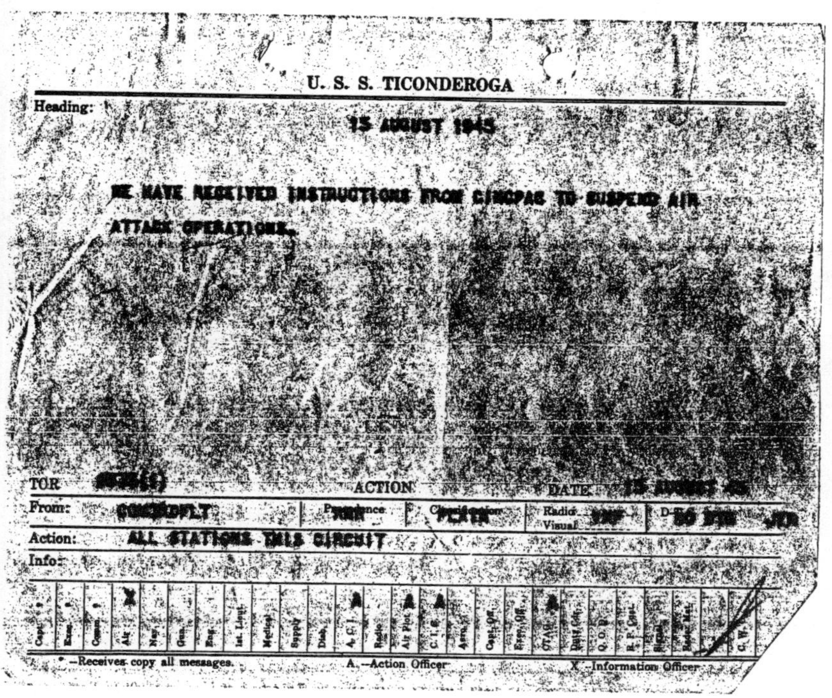

U. S. S. TICONDEROGA

Heading: 15 AUGUST 1945

WE HAVE RECEIVED INSTRUCTIONS FROM CINCPAC TO SUSPEND AIR ATTACK OPERATIONS.

TOR [illegible] ACTION DATE 15 AUGUST 45

From: COMCARDIFLT | Precedence [illegible] | Classification [illegible] | Radio Visual [illegible] | D-T-G [illegible]

Action: ALL STATIONS THIS CIRCUIT

Info:

Capt. *	Exec. *	Comm. *	Air	Nav.	Gun.	Eng.	1st. Lieut.	Medical	Supply	Disb.	A. C. I.	Radio	Air Plot	C. I. C.	Aero.	Capt. Off.	Exec. Off.	OTAC	Duty Cdr.	O. O. D.	R. P. Cont.	Signal	Radio Mat.		C. W.
			X								A		A	A				A							

* —Receives copy all messages. A.—Action Officer X—Information Officer

APPENDIX 3-C

U. S. S. TICONDEROGA

Heading: 142Ø52/AUGUST

THE NIP OFFICERS ARE STILL FIGHTING X THAT MEANS WE ARE STILL FACING THE ENEMY THAT HATES OUR CARRIERS LIKE THE DEVIL HATES HOLY WATER X UNTIL THEY SURRENDER AND ARE DISARMED REPEAT DISARMED THEY ARE DANGEROUS AND NEED KILLING X THE BEST PRESENT INSURANCE FOR OUR FORCES AND FUTURE INSURANCE FOR PEACE IS TO CARRY IT TO THEM WITH EVERY THING WE HAVE X CARRY ON X HALSEY.

TOR Ø754/1 (INTERCEPTION) DATE 15 AUGUST 45

From: COM3RDFLT | Precedence -OP- | Classification PLAIN | Radio 65.34MCS Visual ------- | D-T-G 142Ø52 JLC

Action: CTG 38.1/CTG 38.3/CTG 38.5/CTG 38.4

Info:

Capt.	Exec.	Comm.	Air	Nav.	Gun.	Eng.	1st. Lieut.	Medical	Supply	Disb.	A. C. I.	Radio	Air Plot	C. I. C.	Aero.	Capt. Off.	Exec. Off.	CTAG	Duty Cdr.	O. O. D.	R. P. Cust.	Signal	Radar Mat.		G. W. O.
•	•	•	X	X	X						X		X	X				X							

• --Receives copy all messages. A --Action Officer X --Information Officer

APPENDIX 3-D

U. S. S. TICONDEROGA

Heading: 15Ø2Ø4/AUGUST

CINCPOA COMMUNIQUE #[illegible]'

ORDERS HAVE BEEN ISSUED TO THE U S PACIFIC FLEET AND TO OTHER FORCES UNDER THE COMMAND OF THE COMMANDER IN CHIEF U S PACIFIC FLEET AND PACIFIC OCEAN AREAS TO CEASE OFFENSIVE OPERATIONS AGAINST THE JAPANESE.

TOR 15ØØ(1) INFORMATION DATE 15 AUGUST '45

From: CINCPAC CINCPOA ADVHED | Precedence: PRIORITY | Classification: PLAIN | Radio J3459 Visual ------- | D-T-G 15Ø2Ø4 AC

Action: PACFLT - RDO FRISCO - RDO WASHINGTON - SECNAV...

Info: COMMARIANAS AREA / COM 12 / GHQ SWPA....

Capt.	Exec.	Comm.	Air	Nav.	Gun.	Eng.	1st. Lieut.	Medical	Supply	Disb.	A. C. I.	Radio	Air Plot	C. I. C.	Aero.	Capt. Off.	Exec. Off.	CTAG	Duty Cdr.	O. O. D.	R. P. Cust.	Signal	Radar Mat.	[illegible]	C. W. O.
•	•	•	X	X	X								X											A •	

• --Receives copy all messages. A --Action Officer X --Information Officer

APPENDIX 4

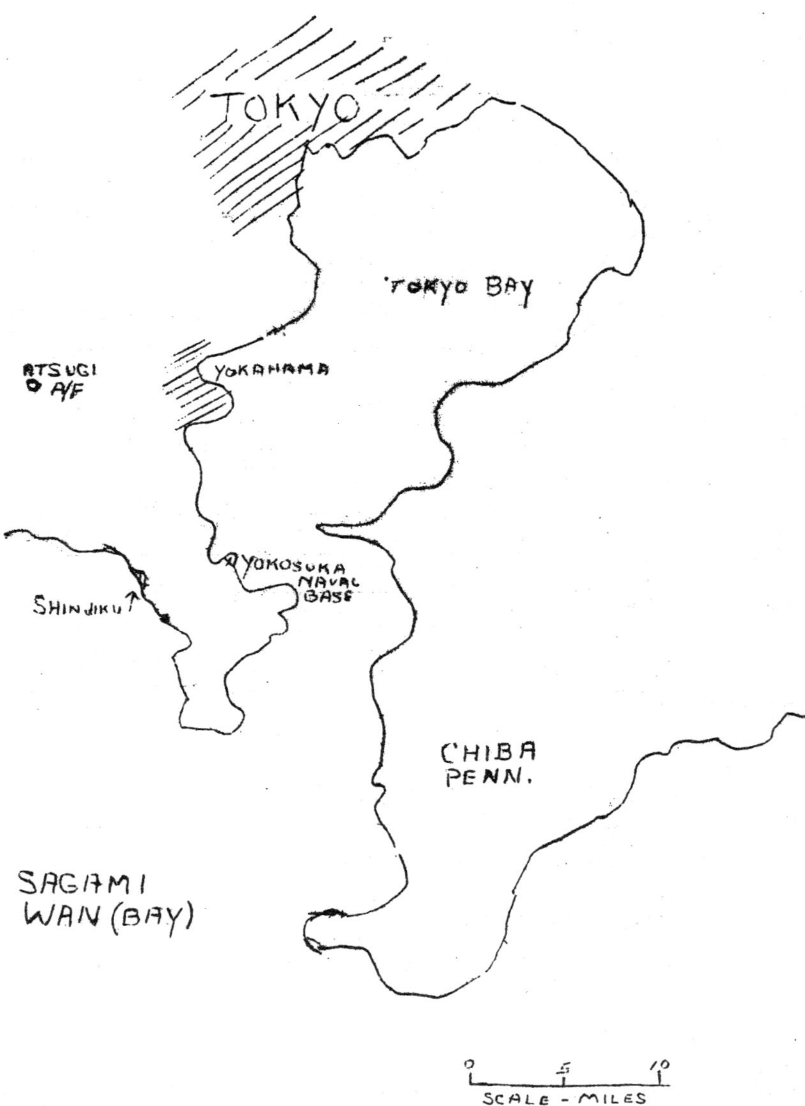

Landing places for advance parties before surrender.

APPENDIX 5-A

Wed
22 August 1945

CONFIDENTIAL **U.S.S. TICONDEROGA (CV-14)**

A.C.I. SPECIAL NEWS BULLETIN

"THIS IS THE CAPTAIN SPEAKING--"

The following information concerning plans for the surrender of Japan and for the initial occupation of Japanese territory has been prepared for the information of all officers and men of the Ticonderoga. Note that the classification is CONFIDENTIAL, which means that neither this memorandum nor excerpts from it may be mentioned in outgoing mail until such time as the story is released for publication.

Friday . . . .

On the thirty first of August nineteen forty-five, presumably on board Admiral William F. Halsey's Flagship, the U.S.S. Missouri, in Tokyo Bay, the event which we all have dreamed of for forty-five long months will take place.

General Douglas MacArthur, as Supreme Allied Commander for the Allied Powers, will accept the formal surrender of the Japanese Armed Forces. The authorized representatives of the Japanese Emperor accompanied by high-ranking Japanese Army and Naval Officers will present to General MacArthur the proclamation signed by the Emperor of Japan, and the instrument of surrender to be signed by all representatives of Allied Nations.

As soon as the Formal Surrender has taken place, the Emperor's Proclamation, together with the terms of surrender, will be disseminated throughout Japan and the Japanese-Controlled Territory.

To forestall any treacherous moves by the Nips prior to the actual surrender date, on the 26th of August, an advance party from Okinawa will fly into Atsugi Airdrome, and Allied Naval Forces will move into Sagami Wan and Tokyo Bay (See Map). On the 28th of August, Army Airborne Troops accompanying General MacArthur will land at Atsugi Airfield, and Marine and Naval Landing Forces will go ashore at Shinjiku Wan and occupy the Yokosuka Naval Base (See Map). From the 29th through the 31st of August, the landings of Marines and Bluejackets will continue, and these Forces will establish themselves in a designated zone (probably the Yokosuka Naval Base) until the Formal Surrender ceremonies have been concluded.

Except for the Cowpens, which will enter Tokyo Bay with our Naval Forces with facilities and personnel for setting up an emergency Naval Air Station ashore, the remaining carriers will fly combat air patrol over our landing forces, and over widely scattered Jap Airfields.

It is believed that the Ticonderoga and other carriers of our Group will fly combat air patrol over certain Destroyers who will be stationed at intervals all the way from Okinawa to Tokyo, for the purpose of providing rescue facilities for the transport planes flying personnel from our bases on Okinawa to the Tokyo Area.

We are all in the midst of events that will make history and you can all be proud of the part you have taken, and will take in it.

APPENDIX 5-B

U.S.S. TICONDEROGA (CV-14)
DAILY PRESS

Page 1 THURSDAY, 23 Aug

LANDINGS ON JAPAN NEXT SUNDAY

....

Radio Tokyo told the world today that triumphant allied occupation forces will make the first landings in the heart of the Japanese homeland next Sunday, Tokyo time. The Nipponese announcement said the allied airborne troops will land only 20 miles from Tokyo and American sources in Manila said the Japanese people would see the greatest display of military power ever assembled on a foreign country. The Japanese announcement said two allied Naval Fleets containing warships and transports would make the second landing on Tuesday in the general Tokyo region east, west and south of the enemy capital. The Japanese announcement came less than 24 hours after the Japanese surrender envoys returned to Tokyo from Manial.

General MacArthur remained silent as to the occupation arrangements. The Tokyo radio said the allied airborne troops would land at Atsugi, 20 miles S.W. of Tokyo Sunday.. Some 48 hours later allied fleets will steam into Sagami Bay which is just outside the city of Tokyo. Then, if conditions are favorable, one fleet will steam into Tokyo Bay itself.

Manila dispatches said every available ship would be mustered for the expedition. Authoritative sources said it would be the first time the full combat force of the Navy had been together for any assigned operation. Besides this, practically all the big transport planes throughout the Pacific will be utilized for taking in the first landing groups. Transport planes are also expected to take in General MacArthur and his key staff. War planes of all types will cover the transports. All branches of the service will take part in the landings.

....

STORY OF THE BATTLESHIP WASHINGTON

.....

The Battleship USS WASHINGTON, commissioned in May 1941, is berthed at the P.S.N.Y. at Bremerton after 25 operations in a total run of 300,000 miles.

The ship's first action was at Guadalcanal on Nov. 1942. That night, with the moon down about 25 Japanese warships moved in to protect shore installations. In a short, sharp clash the WASHINGTON, supported by the SOUTH DAKOTA and 4 DD's beat them off. The great ship fired salvos of her heaviest rounds and in 3 minutes had sunk an enemy battleship.

The WASHINGTON then roamed the seas and in succession saw action in the Southern Solomons, Gilbert Islands, Bismarck Archipelago, Marshalls, Marianas, Pelileu, Anguar, Philippines, the Ryukyus and the South Seas.

In strikes around the Japanese home land the ship fired many large shells and defended herself against many enemy Kamikaze planes, coming through unscathed.

JAPANESE PEOPLE BEING PREPARED FOR ALLIED OCCUPATION FORCES

......

Tokyo also announced the moving of troops from the landing areas in order to avoid any strife arising from the allied landings. Tokyo said Jap troops would be withdrawn from the landing zones as quickly as possible and added that to keep peace in those areas regular police groups were being supplimented by special, as well as Naval Police. Tokyo also told the Japanese people to remain calm and go about business as usual. This was the first word that the Japanese people had received that the surrender envoys had come to Manila.

The Japanese newspapers are now bringing to the people, the cold facts of the surrender. One editorial told the people to face the blunt truth that the Japanese Empire would have to accept the conquerors terms and warned against "wishful thinking" However, the Domei News Agency analyzed the Potsdam Declaration and reached the conclusion that the allied surrender terms were somewhat more lenient than those imposed on Germany. This argument was based on the possibility that the Japanese troops would be allowed to go home after being disarmed and the possibility that they would not be used as labor battalions. This is Domei's interpretation of the Potsdam Declaration.

The Japanese Government also issued a non-fraternization order, emphasizing there is to be no contact between the Japanese general public and the allied forces.

Outside Japan, the surrender situation is also improving. Russian armed forces virtually have completed the occupation of Manchuria and no reports of further fighting have come from them. In China, the Japanese emissaries arrived in Chungking to arrange with Chinese officials for the surrender of the Japanese forces in China. Emperor Hirohito's messenger has arrived in Singapore but the enemy radio there warns that the cease fire is not fully in effect and said the allied forces had better stay away until it is. There still has been some Japanese resistance in Burma, despite the general trend to surrender elsewhere.

....

SUB SNEAKED INTO NEW YORK HARBOR

......

The Navy Department revealed tonight that an enemy submarine slipped into N.Y. Harbor on a night last March and laid 4 mines and escapted. 3 mines were picked up but the 4th. was hit by a tanker which caused damage.

The Navy said the enemy U-boat passed Ambrose Light Ship in a heavy fog and moved to within one mile of the Submarine net before laying mines. When the mine laying was discovered, New York Harbor was cruised for three days.

APPENDIX 5-C

DAILY PRESS Page 2 28 August 1945.

VICTIMS OF KAMIKAZE ATTACKS

The Twelfth Naval District announced today that the Escort Carrior Sangamon and the attack transport Henrico which were heavily damaged by Japanese suicide planes arrived here to undergo repairs.

The Sangamon fought twelve attacking Japanese planes before one breeched the anti-aircraft screen and hit the ship in action near the Ryukyus Islands. The ship burned for five hours after the enemy plane crashed into the Flight Deck.

The superstructure of the Henrico was virtually destroyed when a two engine Jap bomber crashed into it.

ONE ATTACK BURNED OUT 17 SQUARE MILES OF TOKYO.

Seventeen square miles of Tokyo were burned out in a single attack of one of the Superfortresses incindiary attacks last March 10th Doctor Lars Tollisto, former Danish Minister to Tokyo said here today.

Doctor Tillisto said the bombs were dropped over a ten square mile area of the city after midnight but a gale that was then sweeping the Japanese capital fanned the flames through the center of the city until 17 miles were burned out.

AMERICAN TROOPS IN SHANGHAI

The Columbia Broadcasting System correspondent, George Moorad reported from Manila today that "General MacArthur's Headquarters understands that the first American advance troops are now in Shanghai He added "A brief word from that port indicates that Chinese troops are now policing the City which was is almost untouched by the war."

112 ALLIED WARSHIPS SAIL INTO JAP WATERS

Advance formation of 112 Allied War Ships, including five battleships, sailed triumphantly at dawn Monday (Japanese time) into Japanese home waters under cover of swarming Carrier planes to launch the occupation of the vanquished Japanese.

Within sight of Japan's Oshima Isle commanding the mouth of Tokyo and Sagami Bays, the mighty Third Fleet made rendezvous with an enemy destroyer from which Japanese emmissaries were taken off and put aboard the superbattleship MISSOURI.

On that great Dreadnaught were General Douglas MacArthur will receive the Japanese signing of the formal surrender in Tokyo Bay next Sunday. The Japanese representatives provided information and received instructions from Admiral William F. Halsey.

The final arrangements were made in a shipboard conference some forty miles off the Japanese main island of Hunshu for the triumphant entry of Allied Warships into Tokyo Bay with forty eight hours and for the occupation of the Yokosuka Navy Base and Airdrome.

United Presser Richard W. Johnston in a dispatch sent at seven A.M. Japanese time from aboard one of the American warships reported the mighty battleship MISSOURI was flanked by the battleships Duke of York and the Iowa as the Third Fleet steamed toward Sagami Bay to begin occupation of Japan.

JAPANESE OFFICIALS ABOARD THE MISSOURI

A Japanese official party came aboard the battleship MISSOURI early monday as the Fleet steamed into Sagami Bay. They got orders form Admiral Halsey's Chief of Staff, Admiral Robert Carney, for preparing to receive marine and Naval parties at Yokosuka Naval Base near Tokyo on Thursday. This was told in a broadcast from the Fleet by the Mutual Broadcast Company correspondent Jack Mahon.

One dispatch said the slick United States destroyer Nicholas met the small Japanese two funnoled destroyer. The Japanese ship kept her gun muzzels depressed but the Nicholas kept her guns trained on the Japanese ship. A whale boat transferred the Japanese to the Nicholas which then took them to the Missouri. Mahon radioed that the Missouri entered Sagami ~~Bay about ten thirty Monday Japanese time~~ with a fleet accompanying her.

The ships were expected to anchor far inside the Bay in a few hours to await the landings Thursday. Part of the Japanese party were to go on ahead after the fleet anchors, taking instructions for the dismantling of Forts and evacuating the forces. A few of the Japanese are to remain with the fleet as guides. The first airborne landings still are slated for Tuesday.

The main surrender will be signed on the Missouri on Sunday Sept. 2nd. Meanwhile Japan got these further orders from MacArthur:

Immediately after Sept. 2nd, prepare for an advance party with the main sea and air landings there the next day. Prepareto surrender Southern Korea to the United States forces under Lieut. General Hodge on the same date as well as to surrender Hong Kong to the British forces under British Admiral Harcourt. All the forces in the Philippines must have surrendered by then or shortly thereafter.

FIRST NAVY DISCHARGEES GO HOME

The first shipload of Guam Naval men to start home under the Navy point discharge system left Monday. There were 656 Naval Personnel homeward bound.

APPENDIX 5-D

DAILY NEWS
U.S.S. TICONDEROGA (CV-14)
28 August 1945

From: Commander THIRD Fleet.
To : THIRD Fleet.

IN DEALING WITH THE JAPANESE ALL HANDS WILL BE GUIDED BY OUR RIGHTFUL PRIDE IN THE TRIUMPH OF THE FORCES OF DECENCY AND BY OUR OWN SELF RESPECT X OUR TASK IS THE ENFORCEMENT OF THE TERMS ON WHICH JAPAN SURRENDERED X THE JAPANESE WILL BE REQUIRED TO PROMPTLY AND SCRUPHLOUSLY OBEY INCIDENTAL TO THE ENFORCEMENT OF THOSE TERMS X

USE FORCE IF NECESSARY TO SECURE OBEDIENCE X THE JAPANESE HAVE NOT BEEN ADMITTED TO THE SOCIETY OF THE UNITED NATIONS NOR HAVE THEY PROVEN THEIR FITNESS FOR SUCH SOCIETY AND WILL THEREFORE BE REGARDED AS STILL CAPABLE OF THE TREACHERY WHICH HAS HERETOFORE CHARACTERIZED THEIR POLICIES AND ACTIONS X DEALINGS WITH THE JAPANESE

WILL BE STRICTLY LIMITED TO THOSE NECESSARY FOR THE PERFORMANCE OF OUR TASK X MAINTAIN AT ALL TIMES A DIGNIFIED COLD AND IMPERSONAL MANNER X THERE WILL BE NO FRIENDLY INTERCOURSE WITH ANY JAPANESE, MILITARY OR CIVIL, AND VIOLATION OF THIS ORDER WILL BE SEVERELY PUNISHED X WE ARE THE REPRESENTATIVES OF ARMED AND POWERFUL

DECENCY X LET YOUR STRENGTH AND YOUR DECENCY GOVERN EVERY ACTION IN RELATION TO THE JAPANESE.

- -

FRANCE WANTS TO USE GERMAN PRISONERS

According to the Associated Press, the French Officials accompanying General Charles De Gaulle to Washington have said that France wants to use one million German prisoners of war for two years in the reconstruction of devastated cities and lands in France.

The Associated press said the French Officials had stressed the fact that when the European War started the Republic had a population of 41,500,000 and when the War ended the population was about 1,500,000 lower as a result of deaths and the low birth rate.

De Gaulle, the Associated Press said, offered the United States Officials figures showing that it will require 70,000,000,000 man hours of work to reconstruct France and that this was equivalent to keeping 2,000,000 men laboring eight hours daily for four years.

The decision regarding the employment of war prisoners would have to be made by the Allied Reparations Commission with its headquarters in Moscow.

FIVE BATTLESHIPS TO LEAD WAY TO TOKYO

The NBC correspondent, Joe Hainline, reporting from the Battleship IOWA said the Third Fleet was moving in on Japan yesterday and hoped to anchor in Sagami Bay by midnight, Eastern War time.

Hainline reports that the Japanese pilots who are continuing to guide the Fleet into the Imperial Home waters were aboard a destroyer. He said they expected to meet the Allied Fleet at 0100 GMT today and would receive Admiral Halsey's instructions on the surrender of the Great Naval Base of Yokosku.

The NBC correspondent said there were five battleships leading the Fleet into the Sagami Bay, the Missouri, Iowa and the South Dakota of the United States Third Fleet and the Duke of York and the King George the Fifth of the British Pacific Fleet.

PILOT OF FIRST B-29 RAID ON JAPAN IS KILLED

Colonel James D. Garcia was killed ~~here on the twenty third when a B-29 in~~ which he was riding stalled in flight and crashed. Colonel Garcia was formerly the intelligence officer for the Twentieth Bomber Command when it was based in China.

He flew the first B-29 mission against the Japanese homeland in the Yawata strike of June 1944. On that historic first attack, the signal for bombs away was "Betty" after his wife.

LOTS OF MONEY

The United States War Department today announced that in the period from Pearl Harbor to August 1, 1945, 43 months and 23 days, the Army's Quartermaster Corps purchased over 20,000,000,000 dollars worth of clothing, equipment, general supplies and materials handling equipment and subsequent.

This record of procurement of supplies was needed to feed, equip, and cloth the largest Army ever put in the field by the United States. The grand total of all procurements during that period was 20,564,586,000 dollars.

FIRST CIVILIAN PIPER CUB IN USE

The United Press reported that the first Piper Cub Airplane produced for civilian use under the company's reconversion program was purchased today by a group of Indians of the Klamath origin reservation.

APPENDIX 5-E

USS TICONDEROGA CV14
DAILY PRESS
MONDAY, 3 SEPTEMBER 1945

SECOND WORLD WAR OFFICIALLY OVER

The official end of the second World War came when Allied War Leaders and the Representatives of Japan signed the surrender document aboard the United States Battleship MISSOURI in Tokyo Bay Today(September 2nd - Japanese Time)

"The entire world is quietly at prayer at the coming of the new era of peace," Supreme Allied Commander, Douglas MacArthur said at the completion of the capitulation ceremonies - which took place almost six years to the day after the start of hostilities in Europe.

The ceremonies starting this new era in the instrument which the Japanese Government accepted the Allied Declaration proclaiming Japan's unconditional surrender and ordering her armed forces and people to "cease hostilities forthwith".

President Truman, in a radio hookup linking the Battleship MISSOURI with the White House in Washington, proclaimed Sunday(United States Time) as V-J Day and declared:

"With the other United Nations we move towards a new and better world of peace and sincere good will and cooperation."

The dramatic ceremonies aboard the giant battleship reached a climax when Representatives of Emperor Hirohito, the Japanese Government and the Imperial Headquarters signed the capitulation document as instructed by General MacArthur who said:

"In the capacity of the Supreme Commander for the Allied Powers, I announce it our firm purpose, in the tradition of the countries represent, to proceed in the discharge of my responsibilities with justice and tolerance, while taking all the necessary dispositions to insure that the terms of the surrender are carried out promptly and faithfully.

Following the signing by the Japanese MacArthur affixed his signature as the Supreme Commander.

Then he called Fleet Admiral Nimitz to sign as the Representative for the United States.

Next came Representatives of China, Great Britain, Soviet Russia, Australia, Canada, France, The Netherlands and New Zealand.

TERMS OF SURRENDER

Article by article, here is what Japan agreed to do under the terms of the surrender:

Firstly accept all provisions of the Potsdam Declaration.

Secondly surrender unconditionally all armed forces.

Thirdly cease all hostilities forthwith and preserve and save from damage all ships, aircraft and military and civil property.

Fourthly command the Imperial General Headquarters to issue orders to all Field Commanders everywhere to surrender their forces unconditionally.

Fifthly see that all civil, military and naval officials obey and enforce all orders of the surrender with Allied Commanders.

Sixthly carry out in good faith under Allied direction the Potsdam Declaration under which free institutions may be established leading to the Restoration of Soverignty and Government.

Seventhly liberate all Allied war prisoners and civilian interness and see that they arrive safely at debarkation points.

Eightly acknowledge that the authority of the Emperor and the Japanese Government is subject to the will of the Supreme Allied Commander.

TRUMAN'S SPEECH

President Truman, General MacArthur and Admiral Nimitz all paid high tribute to the United Nations ideals and to the people of all the Allied Nations whose blood, work and sacrifices helped to bring victory over the enemy nations.

Mister Truman included in his speech:

"We shall not forget Pearl Harbor," and Added, "The Japanese Militarists will not forget the U.S.S. MISSOURI".

"The evil done by the Japanese Warlords can never be repaired or forgotten." Mister Truman continued, "But their power to destroy and kill has been taken from them. Their armies and what is left of their Navy is now impotent." The President said the formal Japanese surrender is a victory or more than arms alone. "This is a victory of liberty over tyranny."

APPENDIX 6

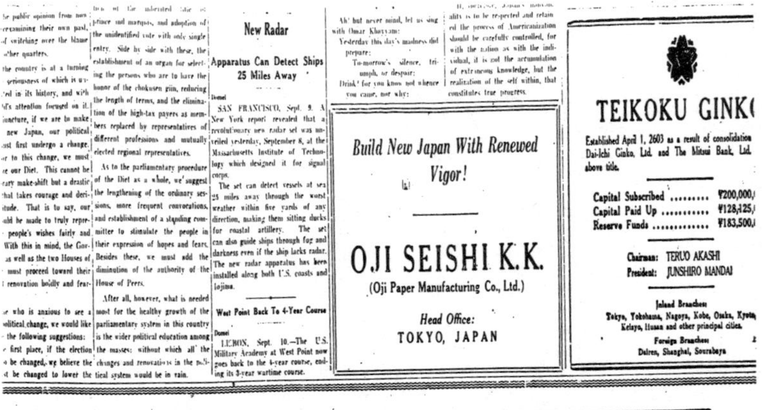

he public opinion from non- reexamining their own past, of switching over the blame other quarters.

the country is at a turning seriousness of which is un- ed in its history, and with d's attention focused on it. juncture, if we are to make new Japan, our political ust first undergo a change. or to this change, we must e our Diet. This cannot be rary make-shift but a drastic that takes courage and deci- itude. That is to say, our uld be made to truly repre- people's wishes fairly and With this in mind, the Gov- as well as the two Houses of must proceed toward their renovation boldly and fear-

e who is anxious to see a political change, we would like the following suggestions: first place, if the election o be changed, we believe the t be changed to lower the

prince and marquis, and adoption of the unidentified vote with only single entry. Side by side with these, the establishment of an organ for selecting the persons who are to have the honor of the chokusen giin, reducing the length of terms, and the elimination of the high-tax payers as members replaced by representatives of different professions and mutually elected regional representatives.

As to the parliamentary procedure of the Diet as a whole, we suggest the lengthening of the ordinary sessions, more frequent convocations, and establishment of a standing committee to stimulate the people in their expression of hopes and fears. Besides these, we must add the diminution of the authority of the House of Peers.

After all, however, what is needed most for the healthy growth of the parliamentary system in this country is the wider political education among the masses; without which all the changes and renovations in the political system would be in vain.

New Radar

Apparatus Can Detect Ships 25 Miles Away

Domei

SAN FRANCISCO, Sept. 9. A New York report revealed that a revolutionary new radar set was unveiled yesterday, September 8, at the Massachusetts Institute of Technology which designed it for signal corps.

The set can detect vessels at sea 25 miles away through the worst weather within five yards of any direction, making them sitting ducks for coastal artillery. The set can also guide ships through fog and darkness even if the ship lacks radar. The new radar apparatus has been installed along both U.S. coasts and Iojima.

West Point Back To 4-Year Course

Domei

LISBON, Sept. 10.—The U.S. Military Academy at West Point now goes back to the 4-year course, ending its 3-year wartime course.

Ah! but never mind, let us sing with Omar Khayyam:
Yesterday this day's madness did prepare:
To-morrow's silence, triumph, or despair:
Drink! for you know not whence you came, nor why:

ality is to be respected and retained the process of Americanization should be carefully controlled, for with the nation as with the individual, it is not the accumulation of extraneous knowledge, but the realization of the self within, that constitutes true progress.

Build New Japan With Renewed Vigor!

OJI SEISHI K.K.
(Oji Paper Manufacturing Co., Ltd.)
Head Office:
TOKYO, JAPAN

TEIKOKU GINK(
Established April 1, 2603 as a result of consolidation Dai-Ichi Ginko, Ltd. and The Mitsui Bank, Ltd. above title.

Capital Subscribed ¥200,000,
Capital Paid Up ¥128,125,
Reserve Funds ¥183,500,

Chairman: TERUO AKASHI
President: JUNSHIRO MANDAI

Inland Branches
Tokyo, Yokohama, Nagoya, Kobe, Osaka, Kyoto, Keijyo, Husan and other principal cities.
Foreign Branches
Dairen, Shanghai, Sourabaya

Do Your Best For Construction Of A Bright Japan!

MITSUI SEIMEI HOKEN K.K.
(Mitsui Life Insurance Co., Ltd.)
Head Office:
TOKYO, JAPAN

MITSUBISHI DENKI K.K.
(Mitsubishi Electric Mfg. Co., Ltd.)
Head Office:
TOKYO, JAPAN

UMITOMO TSUSHIN KOGY(
KABUSHIKI KAISHA
(Sumitomo Communications Industrial Co., Ltd.)
Head Office:
TOKYO, JAPAN

Portion of a page from an English-language Japanese newspaper on Sept. 15, 1945, with advertisements promoting the rebuilding of their nation.

APPENDIX 7

IN DALLAS CO. ALA. PROBATE RECORDS →

NOTICE OF SEPARATION FROM S. NAVAL SERVICE 4672
NAVPERS-553 (REV. 8-45)

BOOK 11 PAGE 220

1. SERIAL OR FILE NO. 2. NAME (LAST) (FIRST) (MIDDLE) 3. RATE AND CLASS/OR RANK AND CLASSIFICATION 4. PERMANENT ADDRESS FOR MAILING PURPOSES
261854
SOMMERS, Samuel Alexander Jr.
Lieutenant (D)
509 Dallas Avenue
Selma, Alabama

5. PLACE OF SEPARATION: New Orleans, Louisiana
6. CHARACTER OF SEPARATION: Honorable — Released from Active Duty-
7. ADDRESS FROM WHICH EMPLOYMENT WILL BE SOUGHT: 509 Dallas Avenue, Selma, Alabama

8. RACE: White
9. SEX: Male
10. MARITAL STATUS: Single
11. U.S. CITIZEN (YES OR NO): Yes
12. DATE AND PLACE OF BIRTH: 31 May 1921, Selma, Alabama

RECORD OF NAVAL SERVICE

13. REGISTERED: [ ] YES [X] NO
14. SELECTIVE SERVICE BOARD OF REGISTRATION: Not Registered
15. HOME ADDRESS AT TIME OF ENTRY INTO SERVICE: Selma, Alabama
16. MEANS OF ENTRY (INDICATE BY CHECK IN APPROPRIATE BOX): [ ] ENLISTED DATE [ ] INDUCTED DATE [X] COMMISSIONED DATE 3/13/43
17. DATE OF ENTRY INTO ACTIVE SERVICE: 12 June 1943
18. NET SERVICE (FOR PAY PURPOSES) (YRS., MOS., DAYS): 2 11 26
19. PLACE OF ENTRY INTO ACTIVE SERVICE: Cambridge, Massachusetts
20. QUALIFICATIONS, CERTIFICATES HELD, ETC.: Gunnery Officer - (C.V., C.V.L.)
21. RATINGS HELD: None
22. FOREIGN AND/OR SEA SERVICE WORLD WAR II: [X] YES [ ] NO
23. SERVICE SCHOOLS COMPLETED: Ordnance and Gunnery School, Washington, D.C. — WEEKS: 10
24. SERVICE (VESSELS AND STATIONS SERVED ON): USS COWPENS (CVL 25); USS TICONDEROGA (CV 14)

PAY & INSURANCE DATA

IMPORTANT: IF PREMIUM IS NOT PAID WHEN DUE OR WITHIN THIRTY-ONE DAYS THEREAFTER, INSURANCE WILL LAPSE. MAKE CHECKS OR MONEY ORDERS PAYABLE TO THE TREASURER OF THE U. S. AND FORWARD TO COLLECTOR'S SUBDIVISION, VETERAN'S ADMINISTRATION, WASHINGTON 25, D. C.

25. KIND OF INSURANCE: NSI
26. EFFECTIVE MONTH OF ALLOTMENT DISCONTINUANCE: April
27. MO. NEXT PREMIUM DUE: June
28. AMOUNT OF PREMIUM DUE EACH MONTH: $6.60
29. INTENTION OF VETERAN TO CONTINUE INS.: Undecided
30. TOTAL PAYMENT UPON DISCHARGE: $ 408.13
31. TRAVEL OR MILEAGE ALLOWANCE INCLUDED IN TOTAL PAYMENT: $ 112.00
32. INITIAL MUSTERING OUT PAY: $100.00
33. NAME OF DISBURSING OFFICER: C.L. BRAINERD

34. REMARKS: Campaign Medals:
1. American Defense Service
2. American Theatre of War
3. Asiatic-Pacific Area (10 Stars)
4. World War II Victory Medal
5. Philippine Liberation (2 Stars)
6. NAVY UNIT COMMENDATION (COWPENS-1946)

35. SIGNATURE (BY DIRECTION OF COMMANDING OFFICER): F. B. SMITH, Lieutenant Commander, USNR.

EMPLOYMENT AND EDUCATIONAL DATA

36. NAME AND ADDRESS OF LAST EMPLOYER: STUDENT
37. DATES OF LAST EMPL'MT.: FROM Unknown TO June 1943
38. MAIN CIVILIAN OCCUPATION AND D. O. T. NO.: STUDENT X-02
39. JOB PREFERENCE (LIST TYPE, LOCALITY, AND GENERAL AREA): Medicine - Selma, Alabama
40. PREFERENCE FOR ADDITIONAL TRAINING (TYPE OF TRAINING): University- Medicine
41. NON-SERVICE EDU. (YRS. SUCCESSFULLY COMPLETED): GRAM.: 6 H. S.: 6 COLL.: 4
42. DEGREES: B.S.
43. MAJOR COURSE OR FIELD: Amer. History
44. VOCATIONAL OR TRADE COURSES (NATURE AND LENGTH OF COURSE): None
45. RIGHT INDEX FINGERPRINT
46. OFF DUTY EDUCATIONAL COURSES COMPLETED: None
47. DATE OF SEPARATION: 24 May 1946
48. SIGNATURE OF PERSON BEING SEPARATED: Samuel Alexander Sommers Jr. — Samuel Alexander Sommers, Jr.

APPENDIX 8

THE SECRETARY OF THE NAVY
WASHINGTON

June 15, 1946

My dear Lieutenant Sommers:

I have addressed this letter to reach you after all the formalities of your separation from active service are completed. I have done so because, without formality but as clearly as I know how to say it, I want the Navy's pride in you, which it is my privilege to express, to reach into your civil life and to remain with you always.

You have served in the greatest Navy in the world.

It crushed two enemy fleets at once, receiving their surrenders only four months apart.

It brought our land-based airpower within bombing range of the enemy, and set our ground armies on the beachheads of final victory.

It performed the multitude of tasks necessary to support these military operations.

No other Navy at any time has done so much. For your part in these achievements you deserve to be proud as long as you live. The Nation which you served at a time of crisis will remember you with gratitude.

The best wishes of the Navy go with you into your future life. Good luck!

Sincerely yours,

James Forrestal

James Forrestal

Lieut. Samuel Alexander Sommers, Jr.
509 Dallas Avenue
Selma, Alabama

APPENDIX 9

LIEUTENANT SAMUEL ALEXANDER SOMMERS, JUNIOR
UNITED STATES NAVAL RESERVE

To you who answered the call of your country and served in its Armed Forces to bring about the total defeat of the enemy, I extend the heartfelt thanks of a grateful Nation. As one of the Nation's finest, you undertook the most severe task one can be called upon to perform. Because you demonstrated the fortitude, resourcefulness and calm judgment necessary to carry out that task, we now look to you for leadership and example in further exalting our country in peace.

Harry Truman

THE WHITE HOUSE

APPENDIX 10

In reply address not the signer of this letter, but Bureau of Naval Personnel, Navy Department, Washington 25, D. C.

Refer to No.

Pers-10 LT-fb
261854

NAVY DEPARTMENT
BUREAU OF NAVAL PERSONNEL
WASHINGTON 25, D. C.

24 October 1946

To: Lieut. Samuel A. Sommers Jr., USNR,
509 Dallas Avenue,
Selma, Alabama.

Subject: Navy Unit Commendation awarded U.S.S. Cowpens.

1. On 11 June 1946, the Secretary of the Navy awarded the U.S.S. Cowpens and her attached Air Groups the Navy Unit Commendation for outstanding heroism displayed by her crew in action against enemy Japanese forces in the Pacific War Area during the periods indicated below:

October 5 to 6, 1943, Wake; November 19 to December 5, 1943, Gilberts: AG 25 (VF-25, VC-25, Part of VF-6).
January 29 to February 23, 1944, Marshalls; March 29 to May 1, 1944, Palau, Hollandia, Truk; June 11 to July 1, 1944, Marianas, Bonins: AG 25 (VF-25, VT-25).
September 6 to November 19, 1944, Philippines, Palau, Yap, Ryukyus, Formosa, Luzon; December 14 to 16, 1944, Luzon; January 3 to 22, 1945, Philippines, Formosa, China Sea, Ryukyus: AG 22 (VF-22, VT-22).
February 16 to March 1, 1945, Japan, Bonins, Ryukyus: AG 46 (VF-46, VT-46).
June 20, 1945, Wake; July 10 to August 15, 1945, Japan: AG 50 (VF-50, VT-50).

2. By virtue of your service in the COWPENS or attached Air Groups during one or more of the periods mentioned above, you are hereby authorized to wear as part of your uniform a Navy Unit Commendation ribbon, one of which is transmitted herewith.

3. This authorization has been made a part of your official record in the Bureau of Naval Personnel.

By direction of Chief of Naval Personnel:

Encl:
1. NUC Ribbon.

Assistant to Director
Medals and Awards.

APPENDIX 11

World War II Aircraft Carriers

Built Before 1939

CV-1 Langley
CV-2 Lexington
CV-3 Saratoga
CV-4 Ranger
CV-5 Yorktown
CV-6 Enterprise
CV-7 Wasp
CV-8 Hornet

Built 1942-1945

Independence-class CVLs—

CVL-22 Independence
CVL-23 Princeton
CVL-24 Belleau Wood
CVL-25 Cowpens
CVL-26 Monterey
CVL-27 Langley
CVL-28 Cabot
CVL-29 Bataan
CVL-30 San Jacinto

Essex-class CVs—

CV-9 Essex
CV-10 Yorktown
CV-11 Intrepid
CV-12 Hornet
CV-13 Franklin
CV-14 Ticonderoga
CV-15 Randolph
CV-16 Lexington
CV-17 Bunker Hill
CV-18 Wasp
CV-19 Hancock
CV-20 Bennington
CV-21 Boxer
CV-31 Bon Homme Richanrd
CV-32 Leyte
CV-33 Kearsarge
CV-34 Oriskany
CV-35 Reprisal
CV-36 Antietam
CV-37 Princeton
CV-38 Shangri La
CV-39 Lake Champlain
CV-40 Tarawa
CV-45 Valley Forge
CV-46 Iwo Jima
CV-47 Phillipine Sea

From: S. Terzibaschitsch, *Aircraft Carriers of the U.S. Navy*. Second Edition. The Naval Institute Press. Annapolis, Md. 1989.

(This list does not include a large number of escort carriers, CVEs, which, because of their slower speeds, operated in defense of convoys and support of amphibious warfare.)

APPENDIX 12

4

UNITED STATES NAVY

heavy aircraft attack off Formosa in the fall of 44 the Japs were dropping aerial torpedoes (airborne fish). Our engineers below swore they heard something clank loudly against the side, the engines are below the waterline. They swore up and down it was a fish which didn't go off. We all laughed at em & said they had war nerves. When I got back out here aboard the "T" the Moo had just come back from an overhaul in the states. I visited the Moo while anchored in Leyte and they said that when she got in drydock at Mare Island (Calif) they found a big dent in the side just the size and with all the markings of a torpedo head! So the Moo got hit by a dud fish while I was aboard. So you see why I'm contented to let the Navy take its time over a little matter like leave. No sir I AINT SQUAWKING!

So much for the horrors of war,

S

Excerpt from February 5, 1946, letter the author wrote from Bremerton, Washington, to his family in Selma, Alabama. "T" refers to the *USS Ticonderoga*; "Moo" to the *USS Cowpens*.

APPENDIX 13

The Montgomery Advertiser JANUARY 26, 1992

Lexington's final departure uneventful

Associated Press Report

PENSACOLA, Fla. — No fanfare accompanied the last departure of the historic USS Lexington from its port of 29 years.

A tug Friday took the powerless aircraft carrier on a five-day voyage across the Gulf of Mexico to Corpus Christi, Texas, where it will be turned into a floating museum.

"It's kind of sad," said Lt. Cmdr. James Salamon, one of thousands of naval aviators who made their first carrier landings aboard the Lexington.

Lt. Cmdr. Salamon made his first landing in 1974. "She was old then," he said.

Its new role will ensure the Lexington, commissioned in February 1943, will get older. The alternative would have been a scrap yard, but the decision to send the ship to Texas disappointed many in this Navy town.

Pensacola was the Navy's first air station, established in 1914 at a former Navy yard that dates to 1826.

Pensacola officials refused to submit a bid for the Lexington because of financial worries and opposition from supporters of the National Museum of Naval Aviation who viewed the Lexington as a potential competitor.

The city, instead, threw its support to nearby Mobile, Ala., which was competing for the Lexington with Corpus Christi and Quincy, Mass., where the carrier was built in 1942.

Shipyard workers in Quincy had petitioned to have a ship under construction named Lexington after another carrier with the same name was sunk in 1942.

The new Lexington was the last of the Navy's World War II carriers when it was decommissioned last year. Japanese propagandist Tokyo Rose nicknamed the ship "Blue Ghost" because of its non-camouflaged blue-gray exterior and its return to battle again and again after she repeatedly claimed it had been sunk.

It gained further fame as the Navy's sole training carrier during its years in Pensacola, racking up a record 493,248 landings before its engines gave out last year, forcing the ship into retirement.

Associated Press

The USS Lexington begins the journey under tow

Thousands turned out for a formal decommissioning ceremony last November, but only about 60 were on hand to watch the Lexington's final departure.

"It's kind of like part of you leaving you when those things get under way," said Milton Branch, who served aboard the Lexington for seven years. "It's something you can't really explain."

NOTES

(Numbered consecutively beginning with Preface)

[1]James L. Stokesbury. *A Short History of World War II.* New York. William Morrow & Co. 1980. p. 378.

[2]*The New Columbia Encyclopedia.* Ed. by William H. Harris and Judith S. Levey. New York and London: Columbia University Press. 1975. p. 1199.

[3]As things happened, I didn't return for a Harvard graduation for 25 years, and then the ceremony was rained out. It was said that it never rained on a Harvard graduation, but that statement was washed out in June, 1968. It poured so heavily that the morning graduation ceremony was moved inside Memorial Hall. There was room for honorands and officiants only. The event was transmitted on closed-circuit TV, but after a few minutes of trying to watch the proceedings in the Lowell Lecture Hall, the former New Lecture Hall, my wife and I gave it up. We did return for my 45th reunion in 1988 and I finally saw my first Harvard graduation ceremony. It rained again, but not enough to move it indoors. The weather, and everything else, was great at my 50th in 1993. The 1968, 25th, event did have an unusual moment. Although the morning ceremony was moved inside, the afternoon alumni meeting was held outside, as usual, in the Tercentenary Theater, the vast, shaded space between Widener Library and Memorial Church. The principal speaker was the late Shah of Iran. During the few days before the commencement, demonstrators opposed to the Shah held placards at the Yard gates. When the alumni meeting began security was tight. Dozens of men, in dark suits, stood at the rear of the stage and at its ends. The Shah began his speech and he spoke, and he spoke, and he spoke. Many of us began shaking our watches. About halfway through the speech there was a disturbance. Several men ran down the right aisle, toward the stage, shouting. Fortunately it wasn't an assassination attempt. Halfway down the aisle the demonstrators were met, head-on, by eight or 10 security men who picked them up bodily and hustled them out the way they had entered. The disturbance over, the Shah droned on.

[4]Stefan Terzibaschitsch. *Aircraft Carriers of the U.S. Navy.* 2nd Ed. Annapolis,

MD: Naval Institute Press. 1989. p. 311. Hereinafter referred to as Terzibaschitsch.

[5]S. Sommers. The author's personal list of dates, places, and operations. A photocopy is in the appendix. Hereinafter referred to as Author's List.

[6]Author's List.

[7]Author's List.

[8]*The Story of the U.S.S.* Cowpens, *CVL-25*. Baton Rouge, LA. Army and Navy Pictorial Publishers. 1946. p. 6. Hereinafter referred to as *Story of* Cowpens.

[9]Author's List.

[10]Author's List.

[11]Author's List. Story of Cowpens. p. 6, 7.

[12]Samuel Eliot Morison. *The Two-Ocean War. A Short History of the United States Navy In the Second World War.* Boston. Little, Brown & Co. 1963. p. 282. Hereinafter referred to as S. E. Morison.

[13]*Story of* Cowpens. p. 8.

[14]E. B. Potter. *Nimitz.* Annapolis. Naval Institute Press. 1976: Selection of strategic operations was by Nimitz, from Pearl, Admiral King and the Joint Chiefs of Staff in Washington, with the approval of the Secretary of the Navy and the President. Pacific operation plans were produced by the CINCPAC staff at Pearl. Local tactics were determined by the fleet commander at the scene under the supervision of CINCPAC with coded reports to Pearl and Washington.

[15]Author's List.

[16]All 1944 actions and dates from Author's List. *Story of* Cowpens, pp. 9-13. S. E. Morison, pp. 306-348.

[17]S. E. Morison, 343.

[18]Author's List. *Story of* Cowpens, pp. 13, 14.

[19]Author's List. S. E. Morison, p. 422.

[20]He didn't get away with it completely. E. B. Potter. NIMITZ, p. 316, says that Admiral Leahy, the President's naval chief of staff and a friend of MacArthur's for 40 years, asked him why he wasn't in a proper uniform. MacArthur explained his leather flight jacket by saying that it was cold on the plane he had arrived on.

[21]E. B. Potter. *Nimitz.* p. 294.

[22]Author's List. *Story of* Cowpens, p. 14.

[23]Author's List. *Story of* Cowpens, 14. S. E. Morison, 424.

[24]S. E. Morison. p. 428.

[25]E. B. Potter. *Nimitz.* p. 328. Clark G. Reynolds. *The Fast Carriers.* New York. McGraw-Hill Book Co. 1968. Reprinted 1992 by Naval Institute Press. Annapolis, Maryland. p. 261.

[26]Author's List. *Story of* Cowpens, p. 16. S. E. Morison, pp. 429, 430, 431.

[27]S. E. Morison, p. 436.

[28]S. E. Morison, p. 437 and following.

[29]*Encyclopedia Britannica.* Chicago, London, Toronto: Encyclopedia Britannica, Inc. 1954. Volume 13, p. 223.

[30]*Story of* Cowpens, p. 17. S. E. Morison, p. 450.

[31]S. E. Morison, p. 472.

[32]Dispatch from *Indefatigable* , author's papers.

[33]For more on armored flight decks see S. E. Morison, p. 541.

[34]C. R. Calhoun. *Typhoon: The Other Enemy.* Annapolis. Naval Institute Press. 1981. p. 89. *Story of* Cowpens, p. 19.

[35]Edward P. Stafford. *The Big E, The Story of the* USS Enterprise. 7th Printing. New York. Ballantine Books. 1988.

[36]S. E. Morison. p. 555.

[37]E. B. Potter. NIMITZ. p. 186

[38]Author's List.

[39]For an on-the-scene report by the Danish minister to Tokyo, see Appendix, *Ticonderoga Daily Press*, 28 August, 1945. p. 2. The Montgomery (Alabama) *Advertiser*, 24 February, 1991. Column by Henry Mohr.

[40]See photocopies in Appendix.

[41]See photocopies in Appendix.

[42]Terzibaschitsch.

[43]See Appendix. Notice of Separation from U.S. Naval Service.

[44]See Appendix. Letter from Secretary of the Navy Forrestal. Statement from President Truman.

[45]See Appendix. Navy Department letter of 24 October, 1946.

[46]For a list of all names and numbers of fast, attack carriers of World War II, see Appendix.

[47]The Associated Press distributed a story, with photo, on January 26, 1992, showing the *Lexington* being towed to her final berth in Corpus Christi, Texas. She has become a museum ship there.

BIBLIOGRAPHY

Stefan Terzibaschitsch. *Aircraft Carriers of the U.S. Navy*. 2d. Ed. Annapolis: Naval Institute Press, 1989.

The New Columbia Encyclopedia. Edited by William H. Harris and Judith S. Levey. New York and London: Columbia University Press, 1975.

The Story of the U.S.S. COWPENS *(CVL-25)*. Baton Rouge: Army and Navy Pictorial Publishers, 1946.

Joseph B. Mitchell. *Decisive Battles of the American Revolution*. New York: Fawcett Premier, 1962.

Edward P. Stafford. *The Big E, The Story of the* USS Enterprise. 7th Printing. New York: Ballantine Books, 1988.

Encyclopedia Britannica. Chicago, London, Toronto: Encyclopedia Britannica, Inc., 1954.

Encyclopedia Britannica World Atlas. Chicago, London, Toronto: Encyclopedia Britannica, Inc., 1954.

Clark G. Reynolds. *The Fast Carriers*. New York. McGraw-Hill Book Co. 1968. Reprint. Annapolis. Naval Institute Press. 1992.

Joe Hyams. *Flight of the Avenger, George Bush At War*. San Diego, New York, London: Harcourt Brace Jovanovich, Publishers, 1991.

Samuel Hynes. *Flights of Passage, Reflections of a World War II Aviator*. New York: Frederic C. Beil. Annapolis: Naval Institute Press, 1988.

Karal Ann Marling and John Wetenhall. *Iwo Jima*. Cambridge, London: Harvard University Press, 1991.

Doris Bernadete. *Mark Twain. Wit and Wisecracks*. White Plains, NY: Peter Pauper Press, 1961.

Nathan Miller. *The Naval Air War 1939-1945*. Annapolis: Naval Institute Press, 1991.

Gordon W. Prange with Donald M. Goldstein and Katherine W. Dillon. *Miracle at Midway*. New York. Penguin Books by arrangement with McGraw-Hill Book Co. 1983.

E. B.. Potter. *Nimitz*. Annapolis. Naval Institute Press, 1976.

George McMillan. *The Old Breed*. Washington. Infantry Journal Press. 1949.

Edward Jablonski. *A Pictorial History of the World War II Years*. Garden City,

NY: Doubleday & Company, Inc., 1977.

James L. Stokesbury. *A Short History of World War II.* New York. William Morrow & Co. 1980.

Samuel Eliot Morison. *The Two-Ocean War. A Short History of the United States Navy in the Second World War.* Boston. Little, Brown and Co. 1963.

C. R. Calhoun. *Typhoon: The other Enemy.* Annapolis, MD: Naval Institute Press, 1981.

John M. Blum. *V Was for Victory.* San Diego. New York. London. Harcourt Brace Jovanovich, Publishers. 1976.

Simon Goodenough. *War Maps.* New York: St. Martin's Press, 1982.

Paul Fussell. *Wartime.* New York. Oxford University Press. 1989. New York. Oxford University Press paperback. 1990.

E. B. Sledge. *With The Old Breed.* Novato, California. Presidio Press. 1981. Paperback. Oxford University Press Inc. 1990.

Colin McIntyre. *World War II, Battle at Sea.* New York: Mallard Press, 1990.

Index